Hadaway Hitler

John Solomon

Zymurgy
Publishing

First published in Great Britain by Zymurgy Publishing in 2007.

Copyright © John Solomon and Zymurgy Publishing 2007

The moral right of John Solomon as the author has been asserted.

Cover illustration copyright © Paul Goldsmith 2007

All rights reserved. No part of this publication may be reproduced, transmitted or stored in a retrieval system, in any form or by any means without permission from Zymurgy Publishing.

This book is sold subject to the condition that it shall not, by way of trade or otherwise, be lent, resold, hired out or otherwise circulated without the publisher's prior consent in any form of binding or cover other than that in which it is published and without a similar condition being imposed on the subsequent purchaser.

A CIP catalogue record for this book is available from the British Library.

Some names have and events have been altered for dramatic purposes.

Printed and bound by Athenaeum Press, Gateshead, U.K.

ISBN 978-1903506-295

10 9 8 7 6 5 4 3 2 1

Zymurgy Publishing
Newcastle upon Tyne

Dedication

To Jonathan, Andrew and William,
my three wonderful sons plus my dear siblings 'Our Joan' and 'M.B.B. –Gordon'.

Acknowledgement

Jo Peel – for her invaluable influence and input (yet again!)

Contents

Introduction 9

1 The Blaydon Lad 13

2 The Courier! 37

3 The Dolly Girls 51

4 War On Both Fronts! 59

5 The Salesman 79

6 Santa Who? 87

7 The Picture Hoose! 97

8 Celebrations 107

9 The Apache Trail 123

10 The Un-co-operative Society? 141

11 Fun and Games in the Pew 175

12 St James' Park 185

Epilogue 195

John Solomon

John Solomon was born in 1934 in Blaydon-on-Tyne. He worked for Procter & Gamble from 1957 until 1977, when he became a business consultant before taking early retirement in 1985. He became the happiest man alive when he married Judy on 16 December 1961. They have three sons and live in Pinner, Middlesex. His main obsessions are Newcastle United and chess, both of which contrive to have similar characteristics – brilliant attack play and lousy defence!

Also by John Solomon

Soapy Business

(also published by Zymurgy)

'Saturday morning was come and all summer world was bright and fresh with life.

There was a song in every heart; and if the heart was young the music issued at the lips.

There was cheer in every face and a spring in every step.

The locust trees were in bloom and the fragrance of blossom filled the air.'

The Adventures of Tom Sawyer

Mark Twain

Introduction

Some four miles west of the great city of Newcastle and crossing the bridge at Scotswood and bearing right is located the small town of Blaydon-on-Tyne.

A newcomer driving through the region, could be forgiven for missing the centre of the town completely, for Blaydon has no town centre! Within the blink of an eye, the traveller is past St Cuthbert's church and, on negotiating a roundabout, soon disappears towards the west and the upper reaches of the Tyne valley. Blaydon is now only a collection of sloping terraced streets descending towards St Cuthbert's church and a cunningly hidden tiny shopping precinct, all surrounded by a sprawling collection of small industrial factory units. The metamorphosis of Blaydon is complete.

However, despite the dramatic transformation of the town which occurred in the 1960s, it is still surprisingly possible for a visitor to take a short promenade out of town and, heading west, soon leave urban life behind to enjoy nature in fields and woodland, something I loved to do as a child. For me, the very name of the famous Geordie town of Blaydon still generates evocative and joyous memories of the fun and adventures I experienced growing up there as a young lad, in many respects totally unaffected by the Second World War; a time during which we as children regarded the hostilities as a great side-show. With little adjustment needed on our part we easily adapted to living with black-outs and rationing and just got on with our lives. Indeed, from our young perspective, the war was really the responsibility of the grown ups!

John Solomon
Autumn 2007

Chapter One

The Blaydon Lad

A siren wailed through the air. I had already been tucked up in bed by my mam when the sound of the mournful and chilling local air-raid klaxon began warning us of yet another disturbed night ahead. This was the tenth night in a row that the dreaded klaxon had reminded us all that the enemy was still intent on demolishing and crushing us. My mam had only just gone down the stairs, and she quickly hurried back up to gather my sister and myself. As she closed the door of the small cupboard under the stairs behind her – where we were taking refuge that night – my sister Joan 'tut-tutted' as I wriggled beside her, and exclaimed that I had taken up some of her space. My mam tapped her legs with a large knitting needle and said, 'Pack it up, don't you know there's a war going on out there?' before starting to knit at great speed, well on the way to finishing another pair of huge woollen socks for a brave 'Tommy' somewhere in France or Belgium.

We soon settled down; my sister trying to read her comic by candlelight. Suddenly there was the muffled 'clump, clump' of bombs hitting the ground. From the sounds of it, it seemed that the target was not the Tyne shipyards some distance away, but close to home.

Not long after the bombing started, my dad crowded into the cupboard, dressed proudly in his rough khaki Home Guard uniform and tin helmet, to check on how we were. 'The buggers have just bombed the coke works in Blaydon Burn and they've flattened most of Twizzle Avenue,' he told us grimly. This was only a mile away! After about an hour, the siren called out its 'All Clear', waking me up. After so many nightly bombings, I tried to sleep when I could. Joan and I went back upstairs to bed, but by this time I was wide awake. I lay in bed imagining I was in a Spitfire, turning and twisting through the sky, shooting down one enemy plane after another...

I awoke with a start: my dream of Spitfires and exploding planes shattered by a burst of loud and bone-rattling snoring coming from my parents' bed next to me.

Several months before I had moved from the double bed in the back bedroom, which I had shared with my elder sister Joan, to the single bed moored next to my parents' double bed in the large front room. I was told that Joan needed more space, and as a reward for moving, my mam said I could have not only an extra potted-meat sandwich for my tea (my favourite homemade treat) but also the extra luxury of my father's heavy Home Guard greatcoat for my bed (for further warmth against the current freezing winter). Ever since moving to my parents' bedroom, I had often attempted to interpret the various snorts and rumblings from my dad's night-time range of noises, which included a high-pitched nasal whistle, often followed by a short drum-like rattle, and an alarming buffalo-like groaning!

This morning, however, I had been woken by a real wildlife gem – the sounds reminding me of the many different types of birds I came across when bird's-nesting. The noises ranged from the booming of the bittern, to the gentle 'tick, tick' of a wren and the haunting cry of a corncrake. Not once was there a break in this dawn chorus, except for the few times when my dad was kicked by my mam, which would cause him to snort and then stop only for a few seconds. To make things worse, the two jackdaws in the chimney of the terraced house opposite began their early morning chat: 'Tchook, tchook, tchack!' followed by a friendly jostling and pecking as they groomed each other. (I was always amazed how their jet black plumage shone, glinting in the morning sun – it seemed to me that they could not possibly be the dirty birds everyone said they were, despite their everyday frolics involving jumping in and out of sooty and smoke-filled chimneys. My own theory was that the jackdaw must have been a bird of quite light feathers, but that over the years, because of its habitat, it had changed into a member of the coal-black crow family – the grey, silvery head the only trace of a once light plumage.)

I had moved into my parents' bedroom when I was eight years old. We lived at number 27 Mary Street, which was on a steep slope and set within the sound of the bells of St Cuthbert's. However, I had been born at midnight on the 28th August 1934 in the bedroom above my grandparents' fish-and-chip shop several roads away from Mary Street. My family included my mam, Dad and my elder sister Joan, who was very musical. My dad was called Jake (he worked as a bricklayer) and my mam was Dorothy, or 'Dot' as she was known. I had heard that they had created a stir in the town a few years ago when they had eloped to Gretna Green on my dad's Norton motorcycle – an event that even made it into the local paper. This daring episode – which I had been told by my sister included the use of a ladder to help Mam escape from her home in Theresa Street – was never mentioned by my parents to me, though I could tell it must have been a really bold adventure. My sister said that the headlines in the local paper ran along the front page: 'Blaydon Lad Marries Brick of a Girl' with an article on their daring and exciting exploits, plus interviews from both sets of parents (my mam's dad, a firm Protestant, was supposed to have disapproved heartily of the 'pagan' ceremony). My sister added that just below this article was a separate story on the winner of the paper's puzzle competition, with the headline 'Local Blaydon Woman Wins "DREAM" Garden Shed'. Beside this was a photograph of a large plump lady in her pinny, with her hair in curlers, standing outside her backyard gate.

I thought the prize of a shed must have puzzled the locals who, along with the winner, lived in a small bunch of terraced houses in the poorest part of town known as Blaydon Spike. My mam had told me that the name Blaydon Spike referred to captured Russian guns brought back to this country after the Crimean War to be spiked. The locals of Blaydon Spike lived in nasty, tiny, cramped terraced houses with the only source of fresh water coming from outside taps in their backyards. They had to share communal privies, which were on some wasteland a few yards from the backs of their houses. They also lived next to one of the largest employers in the town – the Fison's Chemical Company Limited'. The yellow smelly fumes that belched forth from it's chimneys meant that no green plants grew anywhere near the grounds of the factory. Because of this, and their small cramped homes, I thought that the 'dream' garden shed would have been totally useless.

*   *   *

My dad had a great sense of humour and adventure and was often the source of many practical jokes. His friend Eddie Jordan (who was an amazing billiards player – it was rumoured that he slept with his cue at night, chalking its tip before falling asleep and dreaming of his next opponent on the green baize) had once told me about a time when my dad had played a prank on the new local police sergeant, which had involved the local fishmonger (Mr Fletcher) selling to him the monster centrepiece of his shop's open window display – a huge cod.

Eddie said that at this time the new police officer (Sergeant Hudspith) had only just started working in Blaydon, and in true sheriff style (but not packing six guns) had set out to clean up town. Sergeant Hudspith, so Eddie said, began to clamp down on all outdoor gambling (much to the anger of the local men). One popular game 'pitch and toss' (where a couple of coins are thrown against a wall and you have to guess which way up they will land) was often played in back alleys, and the biggest game took place religiously every Sunday morning in the allotments next to the town's rubbish tip.

Eddie said that my dad had decided it was high time someone brought Sergeant Hudspith down to size and so he, along with a couple of mates, decided to use the monster cod to play a joke on the policeman.

So having paid and arranged for the huge fish to be left in Mr Fletcher's window display until he was ready to collect it, my dad then waited across the road from the fishmonger's one lunchtime, waiting for a signal from his friends that would warn him of the approaching Hudspith as he made his rounds of Church Street. Twirling his truncheon and nodding to the few shoppers who looked his way, the policeman soon reached the Co-op grocery store, opposite Fletcher's the fishmonger. My dad then made his move and deliberately brushed past the constable in a shifty manner. Sergeant Hudspith was immediately suspicious of such odd behaviour – Dad had his cap tightly pulled down over his brow and his coat collar turned upwards and had sprinted away from Sergeant Hudspith across the road with several furtive glances. On reaching the open window display of Fletcher's shop, and with several more shifty glances, my dad then reached into the fishy display, grabbed the huge cod and scarpered off down the street to the shouts (from his mates) of 'Thief! Thief! Stop Thief!'

Sergeant Hudspith immediately ran after my dad, truncheon at the ready; blasting on his whistle. He soon caught up with the felon (my dad's 'escape' being weighed down by a twenty-pound fish). Despite Dad's pleas of innocence, Sergeant Hudspith marched him back to the fishmonger's, where a large crowd of Saturday morning shoppers had gathered, some smiling and laughing, others looking quite shocked.

However, when he learnt that no robbery had actually taken place, Sergeant Hudspith was not a happy man, and only reluctantly released my dad – to the applause of the crowd, who by now had realized that they had witnessed a practical joke. Dad then walked home with the monster cod in his arms, handing it over to my granddad – his dad – who of course luckily happened to run a fish-and-chip shop!

Soon after this Sergeant Hudspith left Blaydon (probably to his relief) for a post in Newcastle. The next sergeant to take his place was an elderly police officer who, with only a few years before retirement and wanting an easy life, turned a blind eye to the outside gambling schools (which made everyone happy). Eddie said that he wouldn't be surprised if it had been the 'cod' joke that had been the last straw for Sergeant Hudspith. Such stories about my dad would always leave me wide-eyed in wonder, and I loved to hear them. So, whenever Eddie came to visit, I always made sure I pestered him to tell me more – which he would, especially if my dad wasn't there!

By the time I was eight years old, I had the daily chore of doing any small shopping errands for my mam and gran (my mam's mam Nancy, who lived in the terraced house opposite). Nearly every day after school, I was given a list of any items they needed and I would trot off into town, list clutched in my hand. Apart from the big Friday (pay-day) shopping expedition, which my mam did at the Co-operative Society shops, my frequent errands into town meant that I was a familiar sight to all of the town's tradesmen, and I could easily tell them apart by their different funny habits.

Jack Brunton, one of the town's newsagents, would greet every customer with 'Lovely day, lovely day', regardless of the weather, and the lady who ran Angus's, a small grocery shop (which always seemed to be empty of customers whenever I went in), would greet me with the words: 'Yee've just caught me nicely – aave bin see buzy aal morning with customers, duzens and duzens of 'em!' I also liked Bella, who helped in the Tyneview bread and cake shop (which shared its entrance with the town's only dry-cleaners, confusing many visitors). Whenever I went in to this store, it seemed to me that Bella was always covered in flour and eating one of the shop's many cakes. Because she was the owner's sister she could eat whatever she wanted, and she was always happy to announce how delicious the cake she was eating was, before promptly eating another one!

When doing my shopping errands, I often took a route through town that passed all the main shops, so I could look in their windows to see if there was anything interesting. Once I was past Mr Tweddle's butcher's shop, I would look into the small grocery shop Gallons, a branch of a large chain of grocery stores which were all over Tyneside. The manager of Gallons was a small man, always dressed in a spotless white overall. He was often frowning, unless, that is, the cash-till opened, when a broad smile would appear on his face. He also had a bright red face and silvery hair, and my pals and I all thought that he was the spitting image of the 'bee man' – one of our heroes from the silver screen who could often be seen in popular feature movies seeing off a gang robbing a bank or rescuing a helpless heroine from the clutches of a villain. What we loved about the 'bee man' was that he could amazingly produce a small swarm of angry bees from his pocket and direct them towards the baddies whenever he needed to, sending them running. So, my pals and I would often peek into the shop in the hope of seeing the manager empty his pockets of bees; but no such luck, we were always disappointed!

However what my mam liked about the manager of Gallons, was that he kept his shop sparklingly clean – the floor was always covered in clean white sawdust and the glass-fronted cabinets containing various grocery items like slices of ham and cheese (when there were any) gleamed. Next to the left-hand-side counter stood a stand of tin boxes with their lids removed – my sister said that before the war these had shown off a huge selection of delicious-looking biscuits, which each customer could order with a point of their finger. At the rear of the centre counter was an area that, before the war, used to have on it a pyramid of golden butter on a marble slab; here also there was a large, red-coloured bacon-slicing machine that was so shiny it was if the machine was cleaned and polished after every slice cut! However, although Gallons was an attractive, well-lit shop compared to the other grocers in the town, it never seemed to have many customers. I guess that was why the 'bee man's' broad smile only appeared whenever he rang up a sale!

The shop next door to Gallons was called Gregory's, a tiny family-run drapers. What I liked about Gregory's was that it had a glass-fronted cabinet containing ladies underwear inside, including what my pals told me were stockings, brassieres and various coloured sets of chemises. Grown men could often be seen sauntering into the store for the sole purpose of leering over the counter to catch a glimpse of the latest fashion in ladies undergarments (though I could only manage a rare quick peek before giggling). The drapers was run by Mr Gregory and his sister. He was a slim, tall, balding man, who always seemed to bend forward in a superior manner towards his female customers when serving them. My sister thought he was a bit oily, as he would often follow his customers around the store with a wide smile and a rubbing of hands. According to my mam he had a roving eye and was somewhat crissily (sleazy), and because of this she rarely visited the shop.

The next shop along from Gregory's was the popular Meadow Dairy grocery store, one of several to be found in Tyneside. Most of Meadow's customers had their shopping delivered to their homes and this was done by a fleet of young grocery apprentices on store bicycles, each with a large basket over the front wheel and the store's name displayed on the sidebar below the saddle. The store was always humming with activity, and it had several stands of open-topped biscuit tins to the left as you entered the store (which I imagined would have overflowed with all kinds of sugary treats if not for the war, beating Gallons' one stand hands down).

Most of the staff at Meadow's were young girls with their hair covered up in what looked like white handkerchiefs. They were very friendly towards me and other customers, but would quickly become nervous if the manager appeared. He was called Mr Jackson and he had a sour face with curly lips and a small ginger moustache. He was a regular dictator and often gave the impression to his customers that his job was somewhat beneath him. He had a posh, tight voice and had once told our next-door neighbour Bella Smith that Blaydon was too much of a backwater town for a man of his talents, which were more suited to the better-off department stores such as Fenwick's or Bainbridge & Co. in the up-market city of Newcastle. Rather than have sympathy for him, however, this attitude only made my mam remark, 'Then why doesn't he go there?'

From the Meadow Dairy I would then walk down Church Street past Jack Percy's cycle shop and Brunton's the newsagents. Mr Brunton lived in the posh area of town – Axwell Park – and was one of the few people in Blaydon to own a private motorcar. My sister had told me that Mr Brunton had fallen in love with my mam – the beautiful Dorothy Jones – before her courtship with Jake, my dad. I imagined that Mr Brunton had never gotten over his love for my mam, who had chosen the handsome bricklayer over his own charms (and motorcar), and whenever I went into the newsagents I always thought he looked a bit tragic, like the film star Leslie Howard.

On leaving the newsagent's, I would pass by Lennard's, the popular shoe shop. This store had walls covered with white shoe boxes as well as having many of them piled onto the shop floor. This left only a tiny area of floor space for two facing bench seats, a couple of footstools and any customers. The manager was Mr Kirby – a small, dapper man always dressed in a smart pinstriped suit. He had worked so long selling shoes that whenever a person came towards him he always looked at their feet first, and greeted the customer with either a smile or a 'tut, tut' depending on the condition of their shoes! Mr Kirby was very much a military man, with a clipped moustache and slicked-down, brilliantined hair. He was helped only by one overworked assistant, who seemed to me to spend most of her day in the stockroom at the back of the shop.

Mr Kirby had the reputation of being the fastest salesman in town, if not Tyneside. He was always on the go and never seemed to stop moving. His daughter Jean told me that her dad ate a full fried breakfast every morning in two minutes flat – and this included two mugs of tea! She also said that when he slept, he snored like a Gatling gun. A visit to Mr Kirby's shop usually lasted only ten minutes – if you were lucky. I thought that the record for the quickest sale must have been held by my Mary Street neighbour Tom Smith, who worked as a carpenter in the Co-op funeral shop. His wife, Rita, told me that one day Tom had gone to the shop to buy a pair of black leather shoes to wear for his daughter's christening, and had found himself leaving the store in two minutes flat, carrying a white cardboard box and looking a bit stunned! She said that as he had entered the store, Tom had made the mistake of saying that he was in a bit of a hurry!

Next to the shoe shop was Roberts' the chemist, which was also just next to the Hurst's Company bus stop in Wesley Square. Roberts' was one of my regular stops as I often had to collect my parents' and gran's prescriptions from there. The inside of the store was neat and tidy and to my delight sold (when available) barley sugar sweets and liquorice sticks. Behind the counter at the rear of the store was the dispensary and towering above on a top shelf were several large, magnificent glass bottles, filled with bright, different-coloured liquids, which always reminded me of Merlin's lair in a film I had seen extolling the adventures of King Arthur.

After the chemist's, walking down Church Street towards the river, I would pass the various Co-op shops, which included a drapery and a hardware store, and I would eventually arrive at Sappareti's, the popular Italian ice-cream shop. Because of the war, this shop had shut down, so I would often pass it remembering the delicious treats my pals and I used to eat there. Billie Hutchinson had told me that Sappareti's had shut because the owners were secret agents for Mussolini and had been shot by a firing squad in Stella Woods. This turned out not to be true, which I was glad of because Sappareti's was one of my favourite places.

When it was open, the Sappareti family used to greet customers in a mix of Geordie and Italian by saying: 'Grando to see yee back, bonno lad. Grazi. Noo praego what dee yer want, vanilla or rasperino?' Mrs Sappareti was a large, delightful lady with a warm smile, dark moustache and very fat fingers. If you returned her smile she would sometimes give you free raspberry flavouring or an extra wafer with your ice cream, which was served in a small glass goblet with a spoon. Mr Sappareti was a huge man, always sweating heavily as he worked the hissing and gurgling espresso coffee machine, which often blotted out the noise of the nearby passing railway steam engines. At the back of the front parlour was a small room with cosy cubicles, each containing a table and four chairs. Here, on the weekends, you could see the noisy, older local lads chatting up giggling town girls.

I had loved to go to Sappareti's for ice cream with my pals, as it was a rare treat. With it closed because of the war, I only had my memories of the delicious vanilla and raspberry flavours to keep me going. Dickie Hudson told me that some houses in the posh parts of town had their own freezers, so that rich families could have ice cream whenever they wanted, but I didn't believe him. However, this led me to thinking that if I did have such a machine in my house, I would make sure I ate ice cream at every meal – something my friends all agreed with!

Across the street from the ice-cream parlour was Armstrong and Bateman, the local clothes shop, and just next to this was a public house known as the 'Lang Bar', from which I could often hear loud voices and the occasional bad singing, and smell horrible, beery wafts coming through from the open saloon door. One Saturday afternoon, I was passing the Lang Bar when I saw Les Martin stagger out and, on recognising me, he beckoned me over and handed me a whole, silver threepence piece! With a wink he whispered to me, 'Not a ward, bonny lad, not a ward!' and then turned about and poured himself straight back into the Lang Bar! I stood there, speechless; though not one to refuse such a gift I quickly put the coin in my pocket. I knew that Les Martin was an upright, very religious member of St Cuthbert's choir and on the next Sunday he greeted me at church with a friendly wink and a pat on the head – his beery breath still evident!

On walking up towards Wesley Square, I would pass Fletcher's the fishmonger's, with its open window display. Remembering the story about my dad and the monster cod would always have me looking into the shop window to see if there was another huge fish resting on the ice there. I often saw lots of other fish, such as sole, plaice and haddock, and on the edge of the display there were always mussels and crabs, these last (although quite dead) still seeming to have some surprise in their tiny eyes. Heaped up at the back of the entire display would be dozens and dozens of smoked Callahaan (herring), which were the most popular fish as they were the cheapest, and often sold out first. I hated eating fish, though my mam served it two or three times a week, especially during the war as it was more plentiful. Most of all I hated the fried smoked Callahan, because its tiny bones would make me retch.

To the side of the fishmonger's was a small passageway, which led to Franco Perna's, the town's second ice-cream shop. This was a ramshackled, one-storey, brick shed and its sole entrance was a single wooden door leading into a gloomy windowless room. There were lumps of ice strewn all over the stone floor and cobwebs hung from the ceiling. Franco Perna wasn't a patch on Sappareti's; unable to compete in quality or style. My mam said it was amazing that people didn't fall ill from the ice cream made there. However, Mr Perna would sell directly on the street from a two-wheeled handcart, shouting 'Iceceem! Iceceem!' (he couldn't say his 'R's). I'm sure that the only reason he was able to sell ice cream was that few people visited his work (shed), and so did not realise they were taking their lives into their hands by buying his produce. Sadly, because of the war, Mr Perna had also closed his doors.

Before I would get to Wesley Square, I would also pass by two other grocery shops – The London & Newcastle Tea Co. and Walter Wilson (which had large front picture windows covered with masses of writing showing off their bargain prices). Stuck between these two stores was a small pawnbroker's and Foster's the newsagent. When I was seven years old, I had been smitten by Jean Foster, Mr Foster's daughter. She looked a lot like Shirley Temple, whom I had often seen starring in films showing at the Saturday morning cinema matinée.

Jean had masses of curly blonde hair, a sweet smile and lovely blue eyes. She sometimes helped her dad out in his shop, and although I would always look for her when I went in, I never dared let my pals or family know how I felt. This was mainly because my pals and I had agreed that all females – except for our mams and sisters (and, for me, Shirley Temple) – were beneath us and not worth our attention.

Following a cowboy and indian film that we had seen, the Mary Street gang all agreed to take oaths and adopt names of brave Apache redskin warriors; Black Hawk (me), Brave Buffalo (Philip Lynn), Crazy Hands (Billie Hutchinson), Running Brave (Alan Dodds), Chief Brown Legs (Dickie Hutchinson), Yellow Snot (Dickie Biggins) and Big Wigwam (Fatty Callaghan). We had noticed that Indian warriors considered squaws to be useful only for tidying wigwams, cooking and sewing buffalo hides. We Apaches therefore looked at all girls as less worthy, seeing them as soft and generally stupid. Useless at games and sports, we all agreed that girls cried too easily, dressed strangely and had a mystifying interest in dolls, skipping ropes and helping their mams to cook! They were not interested in football, bird's-nesting, climbing or fighting. So, having nothing in common with them, we by and large ignored them.

Still, I had changed my mind when I first met Jean Foster one weekend when I went into her parents' shop to buy my two favourite comics – the *Dandy* and the *Beano*. Helping in the store, Jean served me herself, smiling straight at me as she handed my change over. I felt a strange, weak sensation in my legs, and blushing for the first time ever I found myself looking down at my plimsolls and mumbling "thank-you" before scampering out of the shop. After that I would sometimes notice her in the infant's school playground, but because all the boys played games separately from the girls, it meant that I never got to meet her unless I visited her parents' shop.

Still, although I only got an occasional glimpse of Jean, I was generally happy just being all boys together with my pals. Then one day at one of our pow-wows on the top of Summerhill (which was a nearby grassy mound overlooking the town and the River Tyne where we regularly met), Dickie Hudson (Chief Brown Legs) told us that a new family had just moved into the house at the top of Mary Street. The family included a strange boy with long hair, whom Dickie had seen wearing a bangle on his left wrist. We were all instantly keen to meet this odd lad, and I was lucky enough to do so the very next day.

I was just leaving Fryer's, a small grocery shop near the top of Theresa Street, on a shopping chore for my gran, when I ran into the new boy smack in the middle of the doorway. He looked exactly like Chief Brown Legs had said, except that, because it was a freezing and frosty late autumnal morning, he was covered up in a big, thick pullover and trousers, a woolly scarf and a balaclava (this last item covered his long hair, though I could see one or two dark wisps of it peeping out). As we faced each other in the shop doorway the new boy made no effort to give way, even though he was smaller than me. A bit taken aback that the new lad was blocking my way, I pushed past him roughly, causing him to stumble. Then I headed back down Mary Street, feeling smug that I had put this newcomer in his place.

Suddenly, I found myself flung to the ground, my gran's shopping spewing all over the pavement. My attacker was none other than 'Balaclava', who came at me with flailing arms and with such intense ferocity that I had succumbed to the surprise attack. I backed off hastily and, giving way, I picked up my gran's shopping and ran off to the safety of my home.

A few days later, after school and teatime, I met up with my Apache brothers on Summerhill and we talked about many things, including a request from Chief Brown Legs that we consider letting in a new member to our tribe – none other than 'Balaclava'! Audie Peel, as he was known, had quickly impressed several members of our tribe with his ability to climb the tallest trees in Stella Woods, ride bareback on one of Howie's milk-cart horses and, most impressive of all, with his raid on Tweddle's orchard, despite the presence of the farm dog and Mrs Tweddle, who was hanging out her washing at the bottom of the garden. Chief Brown Legs had been very impressed with the huge mound of late-ripening pears Audie had managed to filch. With such brave deeds under his belt, we all agreed (me, reluctantly) that he should join our tribe.

Over the next few weeks, the new boy became a useful Apache brother. We climbed trees, raced around Stella Woods and carried out more raids on Tweddle's orchard. Then, one late afternoon, just as we were returning home after a tiring trek from searching for ripe chestnuts in the woods linking Blaydon Burn, the tiny village of Stargate and Stella Woods, we were to get a horrible shock. Happily gloating over our huge pile of magnificent chestnuts, which we confidently expected would form the arsenal for our traditional conker Olympics, involving our school pals and some of the local town lads, we all felt the need to relieve ourselves in the fast-flowing stream.

As usual, Brave Buffalo (Philip Lynn) proved his ability to 'out-pee' his Apache brothers, shooting a jet of around ten yards or so well over the stream. We then noticed that Audie Peel (or 'Long-Haired Wolf' as he had been christened) had squatted down by the riverbank! Astonished, Brave Buffalo knelt down by Long-Haired Wolf, somewhat confused, to ask what the problem was. Then, suddenly, he jumped up and exclaimed, 'Yer bugger! He's got nee willy!' Long-Haired Wolf immediately stood up horrified, pulled up his trousers and disappeared at great speed into the woods, but not before we had all noticed that he was indeed 'willy-less' – something we had not seen before.

From then on Long-Haired Wolf avoided all Apache tribe warpath pursuits. The next time we saw him was some months later, and he was to give us another shock, because he was seen with his parents going to the town's Catholic church, wearing a flowered dress and matching bonnet! Of course, we then all realized something we had never guessed – Long-Haired Wolf was a girl! Her name was Audrey Peel, and she never again joined us as an Apache brother. However, I, for one, took great care in her presence, as I remembered how easily she had defeated me on that frosty morning outside Fryer's grocery shop!

So, with this in mind, it was not a surprise therefore that I kept my keenness for Jean a secret. On my shopping errands I would always make extra side-trips into her parents' store. Then, on leaving Foster's, I would come across a tiny jeweller's shop – blink and you would miss it! The front window of the shop was only slightly bigger than the shop's door and showed sparkling trinkets, strings of pearls and a few watches. Once inside there was only enough room for two customers, and this often meant that a queue would form outside the shop – and even though this might be only a couple of extra customers, it always gave passersby the impression that the shop was very busy. Billie Hutchinson once said that the bright, sparkling trinkets contained real diamonds, so we planned that when we grew up we would one day rob both this store and Sappareti's and then ride west into the sunset, clutching our precious haul and feasting on ice-cream cornets!

Moving along from the jeweller's shop I would get to the town centre, where the Post Office was and (outside of the Salvation Army's headquarters) the town's only telephone kiosk. In the square was also the Station Hotel, the Red Lion public house and several smaller shops, including Shanley's the sweet shop and general dealer (which, because of the war, usually only showed empty sweet boxes in its window, but before all our sweets had become rationed had sold piles of delicious Pontefract liquorice cakes and Sherbet Whirls). However, my pals and I mostly liked Shanley's because the owner's brother, Gordon Shanley, was a famous racing-car driver, whose exploits at Monte Carlo were well known all over the North-East of England.

The Red Lion was easily the most popular of the ten public houses in Blaydon, particularly on weekends when it was crammed full of noisy, thirsty townsfolk. Often, passers-by's would be bombarded with a cacophony of laughter, shouting and singing as the frenetic atmosphere within spilled out through the Red Lion's open saloon bar doors to the street.

The Red Lion also catered for some of the town's most famous characters, not least being 'Darkie Dallas' and Bogie Shields. Darkie Dallas was the most genial of men with a permanent smile, who lived at the top of steep sloping Theresa Street which ran parallel to Mary Street. Darkie Dallas appeared to live alone and according to his neighbour, Mrs Larner 'kept hissell' to 'hissell' and was niver any botha'. Local gossip was that his family had been slaves who had moved from the USA's deep south to Texas on receiving their freedom and worked on a Dallas ranch ever since.

How he made the move from the plains of Texas to the slopes of Blaydon wasn't known, but Billie Hutchinson said that Darkie Dallas had discovered gold in America then travelled the world before arriving on Tyneside and that his front parlour was stacked with gold nuggets. Perhaps, I thought this was why his curtains were always drawn?

On weekdays Darkie only seemed to venture outside his home to shop at Fry's, the small grocers at the bottom of his street. Every Saturday evening he also visited the Red Lion in the town square and on Sunday mornings he attended the Vine Street Methodist Chapel. Always the height of sartorial elegance he wore an immaculate pinstriped grey suit, cravat, matching shirt, spats – (a short gaiter covering highly polished leather shoes) and to complete the ensemble a grey dut (bowler hat). Darkie Dallas was occasionally the butt of an odd comment from one or two local lads – 'Where's yer tom-Tom and where di yee keep yer speer' – however he was respected and admired throughout the town, and greeted everyone with a flashing smile and a 'Hello Der – how's you keeping?'

Darkie Dallas had only one bosom friend, 'Bogie Shields': a middle-aged First World War amputee who propelled himself around in a homemade wheelchair constructed from a small, upholstered chair attached to the undercarriage of a large wheeled pram. My dad told me that the friendship was formed when Bogie Shields misjudged the speed of a runaway horse and cart, and Darkie Dallas had leapt into its path, grabbed the reins and steered the horse away. As a result, Darkie

Dallas and Bogie were a familiar if not incongruous site on a Saturday evening, as they regularly headed to the Red Lion.

Sometimes on my errands I would have to go back up Church Street towards St Cuthbert's Church, and here I would find Pellet's, the town cobbler. Pellet's was a small, dingy shop, lit only by one single gas mantle. The inside of the store always smelled of acrid tanned leather and boot polish, and it seemed to me that the shopkeeper must have been very attached to his foot operated lathe because he only ever left it to take in or return customers' shoes.

Mr Pellet had gentle, kind eyes, huge hands and a tanned face similar to his shoe leather. He rarely smiled or strung more than a few words together at a time; his usual greeting being a single grunt and a sigh, followed by two more grunts after he had left his regular position by the lathe to give you your shoes back. Every inch of the shop seemed to be covered with shoes and boots, some in a thick layer of dust, and there were also heaps of waste leather, nails, tins of polish and dubbin. Dozens and dozens of shoe- and bootlaces hung from the shop shelves, ending just a few feet from the wooden floor, and this was covered in a carpet several inches thick of old newspapers and empty cardboard boxes. My pals and I decided that Mr Pellet lived in his shop, because his gas mantle was often seen burning well into the night, and we never saw him around the town during the day. We all agreed that one day we would be sure to find him under a pile of discarded shoes, which seemed only too ready to bury anyone who entered the shop.

Further along from the cobbler's was Worley's the baker's, a tiny hardware store, and most noticeable of all, the blacksmith's workshop opposite the church. When its wide, wooden yard gates stood open, I could take a peek at the fascinating action that took place inside. There was a large coal- and wood-fed fire in the main brick shed, which, when stirred, would shower a cascade of angry, white, hot sparks towards the tall blacksmith's apprentice. He had massive, burnished, muscled arms and was only protected by an old leather apron and singed cap as he operated a pair of large leather bellows. I was hugely impressed by his strength.

In the outside yard, the gaffer – a giant of a man – was sometimes seen to be shoeing one of the Co-op workhorses. I was always amazed at the horses' apparent lack of pain or discomfort as they patiently stood waiting to be re-shod, surrounded as they were by a madhouse of clanging and ringing hammers on metal.

Once the blacksmith had completed his work, the horse would be trotted up and down by its handler until the gaffer was happy with the job done. Then, with a clearing of his throat, a hearty slap on the horse's quarters and a 'Noo hadaway, ave got me dinna shortly', the handler would ease the horse out into the side lane to head straight back to its comfortable, warm, straw-filled pen in the nearby Co-op stables – a journey I'm sure the animal could easily have made on its own without the need of the stable lad. I always lingered opposite the smithy's gates on my shopping errands so that I could see the drama inside. I loved the energy of the place against the calmness of the horses. However, if I was lucky enough to see the shoeing of the Co-op horses, I was always back home late – an event I would innocently explain away by the length of the queues in the shops!

Chapter Two

The Courier!

One Saturday morning, I was stuck in a large queue (this time for real), which snaked out from the shop Tweddle & Sons – Blaydon's Master Butchers – and spilled out onto the pavement for several yards. I found myself standing in front of the enormous Mrs Waggot, who smelled of body odour and baby's vomit to all who came within a five-yard circle of her (at the last count she had had ten children, with another on the way). She was dressed in her usual black, complete with a heavily stained bodice, and the ragged hem of her dress fell just short of her knees, revealing legs covered in bright, red blotches and vivid, purple veins (evidence of her habit of warming her legs on a cracket stool set too close to a blazing coal fire).

In turn, I was stuck behind the tall figure of the housekeeper from Path Head farm, known locally as

'Billy'. She was built like a prize bull with a face like a goat's (hence the nickname) and smelled of the sickly pong of mothballs and cow dung. My pals and I had noticed she had an Adam's apple which moved up and down like a mad lift whenever she became upset – especially when she spotted us using the rear of her stone cottage back-garden as a shortcut to Stella Woods.

The queue seemed to take for ever to move. Every once in a while, I could hear Mr Tweddle's shouted 'Next!', and we would all dutifully move forward a couple of steps without seeming to make much progress. However, my fellow shoppers did not mind the queuing because they used it as an excuse for the more important activity of high-pitched gossiping, the loud chatter never stopping. I was the only male person queuing, and being eight years of age and quite small, I often found myself lost in the forest of stockings, skirts and rolled-up umbrellas. Yet, even though I was continually knocked about by handbags, baskets and female bums, I stood my ground, bravely holding my position in the queue while letting my imagination transport me far away from the noise of the gossiping housewives.

Above the shop's sign I could see a large, torn, striped canvas awning, swaying and billowing in the breeze, and it instantly reminded me of the sails of an early sixteenth-century galleon, sailing towards the West Indies – a journey I had taken in the company of Errol Flynn and William Bendix the previous Friday evening at the Plaza cinema.

Lost in my adventures on the high seas, I barely noticed how slowly the queue was moving.

The sole occupant of the otherwise bare shop window was an unsmiling dummy pig's head, which (according to local gossip) Philip Lynn's dad had tried to buy for his family's Christmas dinner – although it had been said that he had been topped up with many pints of ale at the time and had to be led away by Tom Baxter, our local constable.

When I wasn't sailing with Errol Flynn, I looked at the pig's head, which reminded me that I was at the butcher's to get some pigs' trotters (if I could) for Sunday's lunch. This I was doing for my gran, who had twisted her ankle in the backyard, and my reward for doing this chore on a Saturday morning was the promise of some of my favourite sweets – Dainty Dinah toffees and black bullets, a wonderful, dark, boiled mint. These were a rare treat and so were worth my standing in a long queue, being squashed and bumped.

At last – after several pirate raids and one full high-seas battle – I arrived at the head of the line and was served by the owner himself, who gave me a wink and a broad smile. Mr Tweddle was a giant of a man, with a ruddy face and bull-like features. Like many of the local shop owners, he was often a subject of the gossip 'mafia' who visited the local shops on a regular basis. This gossip only got worse when rationing was introduced, and the eagle-eyed mafia kept a sharp eye on who got what goods.

By the time the Second World War was entering its third year, we had gotten used to the severe shortage of food that affected everyone I knew. My mam had taken charge of the ration book which had been given out, and which dictated to everyone the amount of many basic food items they could have, including most dairy products, meat and even bread. All 'luxury' items, such as sweets, were subject to really harsh rationing, so much so that it felt like I hardly ever saw sweets in the shops. Generally, except for the odd rare treat, the only hope for something sweeter came from the resourcefulness of my mam, who would save a small quantity of rationed dried milk and condensed milk over a period of time, and make a tiny number of some quite tasty toffees. My pals' mams also did this when they could, but it was never enough to fully satisfy our sweet tooths.

However, rather than accepting this almost sweet-less fate, I became quite skilled at foraging in the hedgerows for wild blackberries, ripe crab apples and particularly sweet pignuts, (dug out from beneath a wild, tall, white-flowered plant we called 'Old Man's Baccy'. This plant could be found in the field next to my favourite haunt, Stella Woods, so I was always on the lookout for its large pointed leaves.) Also from time to time my pals and I feasted on raw turnips and 'tayties' (potatoes) that we would filch from the fields of local farmer and butcher Mr Tweddle. We often roasted these on Billie Hutchinson's homemade barbeque, which consisted of a large metal bucket shorn of its handle, with numerous nail-holes riddling its metal walls.

Mr Tweddle was an important local because of his farm and butcher's shop, and so he was often the talk of the gossip mafia's weekly meetings – or Mothers' Union – held at the Church Hall every Thursday evening at 6.30 p.m. There was a suspicion that some of his customers were getting extra sausages above their ration, which caused great annoyance. Worse than this, however, was the rumour that 'special' customers had been seen coming out of the backdoor of Mr Worley's bakery on Church Street, with 'black market' contraband like jam tarts with real cream!

If these forbidden extras weren't being jealously discussed, then the gossip centred on how the 'special' customers got their bounty. The housewives that received the jam tarts got a lot of flak, and the worst gossip was reserved for those whose husbands were away fighting for King and Country.

The ringleaders of this Mothers' Union gossip machine were my aunty Betty, who had a pencil-thin nose and permanent 'pursed' lips (so that I christened her Nipped-In Bette and imagined she could only eat food though a straw), and her next-door neighbour in Polmaise Street, the chatty Mrs Brown, who talked as rapidly as a Gatling gun. (Even sitting on the outdoor privy, Mrs Brown could often be overheard by passers by rattling away arguing to herself!)

However, I discovered that Master Butcher Tweddle successfully managed to escape the worst of the gossip through his sneakiness and master planning. He only carried out his secret operations by cover of darkness, helped by the rigidly enforced war-time 'blackout' which took place every night. (This was so strict that once the sun had set, even the flicker of a match to light a cigarette outdoors was met by a loud klaxon from the town's Air-Raid Warden and the words: 'Put that bloody light out!')

My discovery of Mr Tweddle's secret operations came through his enlistment of my – totally innocent – help as a 'Gan Between' or courier. One day I was the last customer in his butcher's shop, and, after he had finished wrapping up my ration-book-controlled pigs' trotters in a couple of pages of the *Blaydon Courier*, he had leant across the bloodstained wooden counter and placed a bright, new sixpenny piece in front of me with a wink. 'How would yee like to orn that?' he asked me. I was astonished! Sixpence! A whole week's pocket money! With my whole attention on him he said, 'Aall I want yee to dee, is tak' this note, well invoice' – whatever that was, I thought – 'to Missus Chesterton.' I nodded. Mrs Chesterton lived in Mary Street, just a few doors up from my house.

'But the trick is,' Mr Tweddle continued, 'is that yee must only give it to hor personally, an' to nee-one else, not even hor husband. An' cause it's top secret, ye musen't tell anyone else, not even yer mam! And it must be delivered to hor hand the day.' I was hooked! A top-secret mission as a courier spy plus the bonus of earning an extra week's pocket money – how could I refuse? Accepting the shiny sixpence and the small white envelope, I dashed from the shop to start my first mission.

The previous weekend I had watched a war film at the Empire cinema starring Peter Lorre and Humphrey Bogart, about a small schoolboy called

Pierre. Pierre had acted as a messenger, passing secret documents right under the German SS guards' noses to the brave saboteur *Monsieur* Bogart, the story had captured my imagination. So with this story still firmly in my mind, I left the butcher's shop carefully, first checking to see if there were any suspicious-looking, plain-clothed characters loitering about. Then, walking at a slow, casual pace, so as not to arouse any suspicion, I headed towards Mary Street and my 'drop zone', all the while maintaining a vigilant eye for any sinister-looking strangers.

On the way there, I decided to stop at my gran's home first to drop off her shopping, so that I could concentrate wholly on my first paid assignment – *'L'Operation Chesterton'*. I found my gran in the kitchen, making supper – a steamed leek pudding, my favourite! She had just been getting the muslin bag for the pudding ready when I arrived, and she looked up and gave me a smile when she saw me.

My gran was a gentle woman, who always had time for me. I remember sitting on her knee when I was small and being allowed to press a small, round, wart-like growth on her neck with my finger, just like a doorbell, which I thought also caused her mouth to open wide at the same time! A second push of the 'bell' would then close it. For many years I believed that my gran had a special device inside her that linked her mouth to her throat!

Today, however, I only had time to put her shopping basket onto the scullery table, before I swiftly left with a 'Cheerio! Just popping out to check a bird's nest in the Dene!', intent on my mission.

Mr and Mrs Chesterton did not live far away in the top corner terraced house at number 35 Mary Street, some eight doors up from my house at number 27. The Chestertons were the only married couple in our street without children, that is apart from Mr and Mrs Maughan, who were rumoured to be at least 150 years old each. Every other family in the street had several children, most of whom were of a similar age. Some days going out I would get stuck in the traffic jam of prams that blocked the street, as what seemed to me to be a hoard of proud mothers set off for the town centre to do their shopping.

This huge increase in the number of babies was, my aunty Olive had told me vaguely, because of the blackout, which happened every night to fool any German bombers who might be raiding across the sea. The blackout had meant that a lot of the usual evening amusements happened inside, behind securely fixed blackout blinds. We often had the neighbours over for a singsong around the piano – my dad was a lively, 'thumpy' pianist (having huge bricklayer's hands and spatula fingers that overlapped on the piano keys) and he also gave a fine turn as an accordion player, often setting our feet tapping to his main showcase piece 'Blaze Away'. Sometimes Dad got so carried away by the tribal foot-tapping and hand-clapping audience that he would start speeding up his playing wildly until, often midway through a tune, he would appear to lose all control of his accordion and end up having to dismantle the 'squeeze-box' straps from his shoulders, much to the disappointment of our neighbours.

Such evenings could carry on until well past nine in the evening, a lively change from the usual radio programmes we would listen to. As much as I liked the shows by the comedian Tommy Handley (*It's That Man Again* or ITMA as we called it), the adventure series *Dick Barton – Special Agent!* or Valentine Dyal's spooky drama announcing 'This is your storyteller, the Man in Black...', these had all died away after 9 p.m., so that once our neighbours had gone home we were left with a dull BBC musical concert or an even more boring speech from the Government.

What I couldn't understand was why this would cause there to be more prams blocking the street, and on asking Aunty Olive this some more, she gave me the further puzzling answer that it was because there was now more time for people to look after babies – especially with so many men away in the war. (As a bricklayer, my dad had been called upon to do essential work at the huge tank and weapons factory of Vickers-Armstrongs, along the River Tyne a few miles from Blaydon; my uncle Billy was also doing important work as a fireman in the local fire brigade – so perhaps that was why my own family was not as large as many others' whose men were away at war... . This reasoning got all too confusing for me. Leaving a red-faced Aunty Olive, I went to talk it over with my pals, but none of us could make sense of it. After all, if we had more time, there were a thousand other things we could think of doing rather than looking after smelly babies!

Dismissing these thoughts from my mind as I neared my drop zone, I double-checked that I had not been the victim of any pickpockets on my short journey up the street. Rattling the sneck (handle) of the Chestertons' backyard door (the front door entrance being only used by priests, doctors and posh relatives), I waited for a response, praying that the door would be opened by Mrs C. Unfortunately, the back door was flung open by her husband, who, glaring down at me gruffly, said, 'What can I dee fer yee?' As I tried to think what to say, he added, 'Weel? Ah haven't got aal day.'

Like Pierre, my boy hero in the Bogart film, I had placed the secret document inside my buttoned-up shirt and now, taking a deep breath, I had to come up with an excuse that would get that document into Mrs C's hands. Stuttering a bit at first, I said that I was just knocking to see if there were any odd jobs I could do for him. I added that it was 'bob-a-job' week and that, although I didn't have a uniform as I had just joined the Boy Scouts, I was keen to get started.

To my dismay, Mr C answered, 'Aah! Weel it just see happins thet ah need sum-one to tidy up me shed, so cum in bonny lad and aal shew yee wat ah want!' He quickly beckoned me into the backyard and set me various tasks before disappearing back into the house. Although I felt quite elated that I had gained access to my drop zone, I had not yet seen a single glimpse of Mrs C. As I stacked various boxes and sorted out the shed rubbish, I felt sure that Bogart's brave young courier, Pierre, would have handled the situation better, and already be contacting the target without having first committed himself to the cleaning chores I was now locked into!

The afternoon passed as I worked away, and then, just as I was doing the last of my chores,

Mrs Chesterton suddenly appeared at the kitchen door! With a quick 'hello', she made her way to the outside privy in the corner of the backyard, and then a few minutes later, heralded by the clanking of the 'lavvy' chain, Mrs C reappeared. She was quite a pretty lady, but she was burdened, or so I thought, with an enormous chest, which appeared to wobble independently from the rest of her body (she was well-named Chesterton!). Mrs C also tended to wear heavy, theatrical make-up, with lashings of black mascara around her eyes. Together with her jet-black hair, this added to her belief that she was a descendant of a Spanish flamenco dancer, something that she often told to anyone in the street who would listen.

However, Mrs Chesterton had been born in the nearby village of Swalwell, and as far as I knew had never travelled farther than the Northumberland seaside resort of Tynemouth (twenty miles away) on one of the Mothers' Union annual 'mystery' coach tours. Still, Mrs C claimed that she had once gone to Spain as a young girl and had discovered her Spanish background there. But many people thought Mrs Chesterton lived in a fantasy 'silver screen' world of her own, visiting, as she did, the local cinemas nearly every evening.

According to the Mary Street, Monday morning, clothes-line laundry gossip, Mrs C had started her Spanish fantasy after going to the Plaza cinema one evening over a year ago to see the Hollywood movie epic *Blood and Sand*, a film adventure starring Tyrone Power as a bull-fighting hero. From that moment on,

Mrs Chesterton began to insist that people called her Conchita (although her neighbours continued to call her Connie, much to her annoyance)!

So, with the appearance of Mrs C, I would at last be able to complete my mission. Just as 'Conchita' began crossing the yard, I (partly hidden behind the neatly stacked wooden boxes) hissed 'Pisst!' and gestured her towards me and into the shed. Conchita greeted me with a combination of Geordie laced with a fractured Spanish dialect: 'Ola! Caramba! Jose, what can I, Conchita, helpo you weeth bonny lad?' Reaching for the top-secret document from under my shirt, I was just about to pass it to her when the kitchen door opened and Mr Chesterton shouted out: 'Whet's foor mee dinna? Aas yee naw, I'm off to the pijun club shortly.'

Conchita immediately turned around and, with her chest causing mayhem under her blouse, ran quickly from the yard back into the house. Dismayed, I finished off the last of my chores and knocked on the kitchen door, hoping that Mrs C would answer. Perhaps I could complete my mission now, I thought, but my luck was out. Mr Chesterton opened the door, quickly inspected the now tidy back shed and, handing me a silver threepenny coin, murmured his thanks and disappeared back into the house.

Failure! I was horrified. My mission was a disaster. How would *Monsieur* Bogart and his brave chums of the Resistance have reacted? More to the point, how would the Master Butcher feel if I was unable to deliver the top-secret document today as he had asked me to do? Suddenly the kitchen door flew open and Mrs C emerged looking somewhat flustered. 'Jose! A beeg favour – I have run out of breado, pop doon to the corner shop and get me el loaf and take these pesetas, I mean pennies, and my rationino livro.'

A fresh chance! Elated, off I sprinted down the few hundred yards to the shop and returned, breathlessly handing over (with a conspiratorial wink) the loaf of bread as well as the concealed secret document. With a puzzled look on her face, Mrs C took the package, said, 'Obligatoo!', and then suddenly smiled with a far away look in her dark eyes when I whispered to her the document's origin.

Mission accomplished! I sprinted from the drop zone towards home flushed with my success and now free to imagine what I could spend my by now hard-earned ninepence on. Such wealth could easily buy me several packets of my favourite Dainty Dinah toffees (when they were in the shops of course) or a ticket to the Plaza cinema to share the adventures of Flash Gordon at next Saturday's matinée. Forget joining the foreign legion with Gary Cooper when I grew up, I was going to be an International Courier Spy!

Chapter Three

The Dolly Girls

My mam and her elder sister, Aunty Olive, had between them a unique sense of humour. What appeared to be normal run-of-the-mill things, unnoticed by everyone else, were often for them the spark for a bout of uncontrollable laughter. Whenever they saw an embarrassing situation developing, whether it was in the parlour of a neighbour's house or an unfortunate 'banana peel' incident by some stranger outside in the street, their strange humour would trigger laughter in both of them, often without a word being said. From sniggering at the same time to knicker-wetting guffaws, these bouts of merriment became more lively if they realised that no-one else shared or understood why they were laughing. My sister and I often exchanged puzzled looks when they would set each other off.

Once, on a shopping trip to search for bargains in the large Marks and Spencer on Northumberland Street in Newcastle, Mam and Aunty Olive decided to go to the lingerie section on the upper floor of the store. As they neared the top of the escalator, they both glanced at each other and said at the same time, 'Can you smell custard?!' This would be a strange comment for anyone other than my mam and Aunty Olive, who both fell about in fits of laughter. Their fellow shoppers looked shocked as these two well-dressed, middle-aged women staggered onto the shop floor from the escalator.

The more my mam and aunty tried to stop laughing, the worse it got. Everyone else around them must have thought that, despite the time of day (11.30 am.), here were two disgustingly drunk women and, with much tutting and pursed lips, they attempted to ignore them. Of course, by now both my mam and Aunty Olive had realised that by the onlookers' embarrassed glances and tuttings of 'disgusting!' and 'winos!', they were being totally misunderstood. But further attempts to control their laughter only led to Aunty Olive squatting helplessly on the carpeted floor and wetting herself! Mam, realising that it was important that they left the shop as soon as possible, somehow managed to get both herself and Aunty Olive down the stairs, out of the store and, thankfully, onto the crowded street outside.

Aunty Olive had to immediately make a beeline to the Fenwick departmental store just farther down the street to buy a pair of knickers! But perhaps she should have bought more than one pair, because once she rejoined my mam five or so minutes later, it only took a further glance between them to send them into more explosions of laughter. In the end they had to part company and go their separate ways to the bus station to return home. On the bus my mam sat at the very rear of the coach, whilst Aunty Olive sat as far away as possible in the front.

Having fled Marks and Spencer, the Dolly Girls (as they liked to be called, after a famous sister variety double-act in the Thirties) must have left behind a group of fellow shoppers and staff gossiping wildly about the disgraceful and embarrassing episode they had just seen! I am just glad that I was not there with them, or, for that matter, the poor soul with a mop and bucket who would have had to clean up after Aunty Olive's humour.

Sometimes I would join Mam and Aunty Olive on one of their big shopping expeditions to Newcastle. It was not so much the shopping or the busy streets that I liked (and which in fact I loathed), but the actual journey from Blaydon to Newcastle riding on one of the Venture Motor Company's orange and cream buses that I enjoyed. These buses had a shining silver figurehead on top of the radiator, showing the head of a redskin, whom I christened Geronimo despite the name of the engine manufacturer 'Guy' being written just below.

A fleet of these magnificent vehicles ran throughout the region and allowed for two passengers to sit at the front left of the bus, right next to the driver. I would always try to sit here, and imagined that if ever the bus driver collapsed or fainted at the wheel, I could be the hero of the day by jumping into the driver's seat, putting the gear lever into neutral, applying the handbrake and switching off the engine – something I had seen the driver do countless times.

On another shopping trip, my mam and Aunty Olive were on the lookout for a bargain. I had overheard them telling my gran about their recent journey to 'Toon' or 'Newcarsel-upon-Tyne' as those from the city's high-class area of Gosforth would say. Mam had seen, only a few days before, an ad in the local paper – the *Evening Chronicle* – that was inviting customers to visit the posh department store of Bainbridge & Co. on Market Street. The store was holding a massive, one-week sale – and the item that caught my mam's attention was: 'Clearance of Quality Household Items – never to be repeated! Hearthrugs! Only 4/6d each! (Normally £2 each!) Must Clear! Hurry, Hurry, Hurry!'

Such a good deal easily tempted my mam and Aunty Olive and so off they went to Newcastle on the fifteen-minute bus trip two days later. This time they both agreed to stay clear of Marks and Spencer and instead they made their way through the busy crowds of Friday shoppers to Bainbridge & Co. The carpet department was on the third floor and, with no escalator, they slowly climbed the flight of stairs (luckily no custard smells joined them there!). The whole of the third floor was as long as it was wide and it was covered in stacks of orderly rolls of carpet. Above each display were hung brightly coloured signs shouting 'Sale!' and 'Bargain!', making the whole floor look festive.

My mam and aunty immediately set forth between the rolls of carpet to search for the sole object of their trip into the store – the hearthrugs. Up and down, up and down they went, but failed to spot the display area for rugs. After a while, tired and annoyed, they spotted a member of staff who luckily turned out to be the manager. He was a smartly dressed, middle-aged man with a miserable face and glistening Brylcreamed hair, smelling strongly of aftershave. The badge on his lapel said his name was 'Tarquin-at-your-service', and after Aunty Olive asked him where the special offer rugs were, he told them in a high-pitched, squeaky voice – and with many apologies – that the discounted 4/6d hearthrugs had already sold out!

Outraged and shocked, the Dolly Girls both launched into an angry tirade against the poor manager. In a withering twin attack and, without seemingly pausing for breath, they asked why there was not enough stock to back up the recent newspaper advert. The only reason that they had come on this long tiring journey (four miles!) to the town, was because of the Bainbridge & Co. advertisement in the *Evening Chronicle*, which they had read only the other day. How could such a well-known store deceive their regular customers? What about not only the wasted bus fares but the waste of their precious time? We will write to your board of directors, they threatened! On and on they went, to what must have seemed like hours to the poor manager. (On hearing this tale later, I could only wince in sympathy, having been at the receiving end of the Dolly Girls' tongue-lashings before.)

The manager, Tarquin, must have been at his wits' end and, crumbling visibly, slowly sat down on a nearby roll of carpet, close to tears. Realising the manager had been suitably told off and calming down, the Dolly Girls said 'Good day!' with a final frown and swept out of the department as if on a regimental march.

So, having missed out on the bargain hearthrugs, my mam and aunty left the store from the main Market Street entrance and decided to make for the nearby, popular Carricks Tea Rooms on Grey Street for a cup of tea instead. As they headed towards the café, feeling at least satisfied they had given the Bainbridge manager a piece of their minds, they realised that they would pass the entrance of Binns, another department store occupying the other half of the large, up-market building which also housed their rivals Bainbridge & Co. Both stores had several different entrances both on Market Street and Grey Street.

Deciding that they might as well take a quick look in the Binns carpet department in case they had similar bargains on display, but wanting to avoid the lunch-time crowds in the café, my mam and aunty dashed into the side entrance of Binns to arrive breathless at the carpet department on the third floor. They were happy to discover that Binns were also having a carpet sale, as large signs with 'Sale!' and 'Bargain!' were also hung above rolls of carpet.

The Dolly Girls hurriedly set off to search for the hearthrugs and, spotting a member of staff, they went over to ask him about them. The man had taken off his suit jacket and was mopping his brow with a handkerchief. Dismissing the vague familiarity of the man, my mam said, 'Excuse me, young man, we're looking for the hearthrugs.' His reaction to her question was pure theatre! Leaping into the air like Errol Flynn, he gave a strangled cry and then raced away, leap-frogging over the regimented lines of carpet. The Dolly Girls, of course, in their hurry to complete their shopping, had mistakenly rushed up the wrong flight of stairs at the back entrance (forgetting that at the back of the building both Binns and Bainbridge & Co. had doors to their shops which were right next to each other). Both my mam and my aunty were back in the Bainbridge carpet department – having gone back there from a different direction, they had not noticed they were in the same store! In approaching the manager, poor Tarquin must have imagined the 'angels of death' were coming to haunt him and had very sensibly made off!

Chapter Four

War On Both Fronts!

My on-going apprenticeship in the murky and dangerous world of the undercover spy continued all summer long. My butcher-shop visits with their sly winks, secret 'Chesterton' messages and regular drop zones gave me a steady flow of extra cash, which funded extra trips to the cinema and some Dainty Dinah Toffees whenever I could get any. My fantasy life as a spy (I had by now taken on the codename 'Black Hawk') was very exciting, and together with the extra money (which I spent so quickly my parents were none the wiser), meant that I was eager to carry on with my secret spy missions.

I never once opened the secret documents that Mr Tweddle gave to me and was happy enough with the additions to my pocket money not to question all the 'invoices' I was passing along – or why there were so many of them.

One late Saturday afternoon, I was running through a large, freshly-cut hayfield on my way to check a partridge's nest that I had discovered recently near Stoney's pond. Dotted throughout the field (which was owned by the Tweddle family) were dozens and dozens of large haystacks. As I ran through the straw gauntlet, pretending that hidden behind each one was an SS German sniper, I soon neared the edge of the field and suddenly came upon two adults in a surprising 'clutch'. Nestled at the base of a haystack, their rolling bodies were locked together and their faces were partly covered in the deep straw. In my one and only short glimpse – I hurried on in surprise – I was sure I saw the huge bulk of Master Butcher Tweddle with his noticeable heavy red neck and grey curly hair and a strange, moaning woman who had long, dark hair and very dark eyes! Sprinting to the nearby five-bar gate, I climbed over and made my way to Stoney's pond, puzzling over the strange behaviour of adults.

I had been dropping off secret documents for several weeks now, but soon after my trip through the hayfield my 'target' changed from Mrs C to the wife of the manager of the Plaza cinema, Mrs Tindall – or 'Dorothy Lamour' as we called her, because she was an attractive, glamorous lady like the famous Hollywood film star, always dressed up in furs (some of which had heads still attached to them). According to Alan Dodds's elder brother, Mrs Tindall and the film star must have been related, as both had the same thick, red lips and identical 'come-to-bed' eyes. (This phrase we were unsure about, until another member of our gang – Dickie Biggins – explained that he thought it meant a woman's sign that she was tired and ready for sleep, which seemed to make sense to us all.)

I did not think much about my changed drop zone until some months later when I overheard my mam and aunty talking (gossiping) about the separation of our neighbours, the Chestertons. Mr Chesterton had gone off to live with his mam and they wondered whether Connie Chesterton had left the area completely to go to Seville to join up with a Spanish bullfighter. This was something that 'Conchita' herself had said over a cup of tea with the Mothers' 'gossip' Union's leading committee member – the eyes and ears of the town – the busybody Mrs Brown, probably knowing it would soon spread throughout Blaydon.

However, such gossip did not make a huge impression on me, as I was busy in my role as International Courier Spy, successfully slipping to and from my new drop zone – the Plaza manager's posh house in Axwell Park – unnoticed.

Billie Hutchinson, Alan Dodds, Dickie Biggins, Dickie Hudson, Philip Lynn and myself (alias 'Black Hawk') were the core of the Mary Street gang. We regularly played together and could often be seen in one of our favourite haunts, Stella Woods. After seeing a really entertaining cowboys and indians film at the Plaza cinema one week, we all decided to follow the Apache custom that had been shown during the movie, and form a true friendship between us by becoming blood brothers. Meeting on the summit of Summerhill, we drew straws to decide who would go first in the blood-binding ceremony. As luck would have it (for the rest of us), Dickie Biggins and Philip Lynn both drew the short straws.

While Dickie Hudson, Alan, Billie and myself blew sighs of relief, we squatted on the grass banging sticks together and chanting like true Apache warriors, waiting for the initiation ceremony to begin. Philip Lynn was always the most daring of the gang – he had once trespassed into Tweddle's orchard, with their fierce sheepdog dozing just by the fruit tree, and had filched a dozen, large, green 'cooker' apples, which we ate ravenously (though the next day, Billie Hutchinson wasn't able to come out to play). Philip Lynn also gained our further admiration because he had once peed on a wasps' nest he had discovered in the undergrowth, whilst hunting for birds' nests in Stella Woods and, although he was stung on his private parts, he never once cried!

So, it was without surprise that I saw Philip baring his arm and brandishing the ceremonial blade – a large, fearsome meat-carving knife that Alan Dodds (whom we called 'Running Brave' as he was the best runner in the gang) had bravely smuggled from his mam's cutlery box. Philip beckoned Dickie to roll up his shirtsleeve also, but Dickie went as white as a sheet and, with a suspicion of tears, chickened out, mumbling that he had forgotten to run an errand for his mam. He then leapt up and ran down Summerhill in the direction of home.

We were appalled! A coward in the gang! The rest of us leapt up and with Apache war cries scampered after him. Secretly, the rest of us were, of course, relieved that the escaping Dickie had put off the initiation ceremony, although Philip Lynn was annoyed that in our stampede to capture the fleeing coward, he had accidentally dropped the carving knife into the burn whilst crossing the footbridge over it. Running Brave despaired over this and we decided never to speak to Dickie Biggins again. However, we did go to his birthday party the following weekend – his mam having laid out potted-meat sandwiches, jam tarts and Tizer for the celebratory tea – but he was automatically banned from all gang activities from then on. Good riddance anyway, we thought – until his next birthday, that is!

After wartime rationing began, we were always famished and food occupied our thoughts more than anything else. Anything we could find to help sate our gnawing hunger between meal times and to add to our tiny home rations was a bonus – we would often scavenge from the local fields and woods for wild fruit and Tweddle's farm-cultivated root vegetables. My mam, like most of the other housewives, now had to use all of her skills to feed and clothe us, often swapping clothing coupons with a neighbour for their meat or bread equivalent, so that we could have a variety of food on the table. However, it never seemed enough, and I often left the table still hungry.

Once my sister was severely told off by our mam for having had the nerve to ask for an extra pat of butter (Mr Bumble, the ferocious parish beadle from the film *Oliver Twist* had nothing on her!). As time went on, we were even served with whale meat, black bread and horrible tripe in a revolting milk sauce, none of which satisfied my young appetite – more because I rejected all persuasion and threats to try more than a mouthful of this truly awful-tasting food, despite my hunger.

On good days, my mam would sometimes give me an extra slice of bread (my normal ration for afternoon tea was one slice), which, fried with several pigeons' eggs, was quite delicious and tasted similar to hens' eggs, only much sweeter. We were lucky to get the eggs from my dad's racing-pigeon loft (or ducket as they were known locally). My dad and granddad were fanatical racing-pigeon fanciers and Dad only grudgingly gave up his pigeons' eggs on the rare occasions he was forced to.

One of the few times I ever saw Dad get angry was one evening when Mam (who was becoming more and more concerned about the lack of food in the larder) hesitantly suggested, after an especially frugal meal, that perhaps Dad would consider offering a couple of his precious racing pigeons to bulk up the rations for the rest of the week. Oh dear! Dad exploded! I didn't know anyone who was more keen about pigeon racing, other than my granddad that is. Together, they shared a terrific passion for this hobby, which was more important than all other family and sporting occasions. His birds numbered well into the fifties and he gave them all his attention. While he refused to lift a broom or a cloth at home, the pigeon loft was religiously cleaned, often twice daily. The spoiled birds were fed, watered and exercised every day without fail, and I often helped out before and after school.

All this devotion also came with a history of success in pigeon racing. Solomon & Son had the reputation as one of the most successful racing-pigeon lofts in the region, and were winners of many local and national trophies.

'Bloody pigeons!' my dad now exclaimed with a rising voice. 'Dee ye nah hoo many years ave spent trainin' 'em? Weel afor we met!' he continued, getting angrier by the second. 'Aah wark hard every day and bring in gud wages each Friday and mee only pleasure is mee pigeons. Aaad rather cut off mee arm and roast it, afore harmin' a feather of me burds!' and with this he stalked off out of the house. Poor Mam burst into tears and my sister and I tried our best to comfort her (though all the time I was wondering what a roasted arm would taste like!).

My mam didn't have to worry so much about vegetables, however, because Dad had an allotment, which gave us a regular supply. Unfortunately I loathed cabbages and sprouts, and drove my mam to distraction by my self-imposed diet. I would often be forced to remain sitting at the table after everyone else had finished eating, gazing mournfully at the unfinished food on my plate. I would end up picking over this – despite my hunger, I could not force it down – for up to twenty or thirty minutes before Mam, depending on her mood, would relent and let me out of the house or send me packing off to bed. Nothing, but nothing, would get me to eat a single sprout!

My favourite outdoors hobby was to search for bird nests. I had clambered all around Blaydon for many years, spotting out the nesting places of many local birds. I would often have to remain still, squatting cramped for long periods of time huddled in the dark undergrowth to discover a particular bird's flight approach, which would then let me track down the location of its nest, or in the case of the skylark, the cunning approach to its home hidden on the ground. I loved to watch the skylark swooping down to earth from a great height, and then run around in several directions as a distraction before arriving at its nest concealed in the meadow grass.

During the spring nesting season, I would scamper out of the house immediately after tea and head for Stella Woods and the surrounding countryside some two miles away. I would often lose all sense of time there. Only the falling darkness would recall me to the time, ending that day's bird hunt in the woods. Climbing down the branches of a fir tree, after trying to find the elusive crossbill's nest, I would often trek back home alone, happy with my thoughts of the discoveries I had made that day.

I liked to be on my own when on my bird-spotting quests and I did not wish to share my triumphant discoveries with anyone else or risk the complete clutches of birds' eggs being stolen. This was very common, and when I came across a recently discovered nest where all the eggs had obviously been taken, such evidence of 'huggying' often broke my heart. My sad thoughts always turned to the parents and their grief, for I imagined that after the loss of their eggs, the parents never sang again.

Whenever I did discover a nest, I made sure I had not been followed by a 'huggier'. If I visited a nest location regularly, I would often attempt to fool the would-be 'huggiers' by adding extra foliage as camouflage to the entrance of the nest. Also, when the hen bird had completed its complete clutch of eggs, I always made sure I only removed one egg from the nest to add to my collection, which was one of my prized possessions. The centrepiece of my collection however was not from a local bird. My gran had once travelled to Australia on the *Cutty Sark* when she was a small girl, and returned with her family to England after only a couple of years (their time on the far side of the world not being a success). One of the things she had brought back with her was an emu's egg, which she later gave to me for my collection. I was overjoyed with this because not only was it the largest egg of all the ones I owned, it was also the envy of all my friends.

So, even though I was often out and about on my own, bird's-nesting sometimes until very late, my parents let me range freely around the local area. We lived in a neighbourhood without any serious crime, indeed, the only danger to me was either falling from a tree or slipping down a clay bank into the stream flowing through Stella Woods. A mere nothing to a hardy bird hunter! Despite the war raging in Europe, and the now common blackout in force every night (which I found exciting!), I regularly set out for up to five hours to comb the local area for bird nests.

In fact, such was the lack of severe crime locally, that the only time the local police cell saw any business was when an over-excited drunk got noisy on a Saturday night in the town square (and this was often one of the main sources of gossip for the traditional, Monday morning, washing-line brigade!).

Our next-door neighbour was Mrs Knight, or 'Fadge' as I christened her, because her podgy face reminded me of the large, round loaf of bread baked locally. Fadge would often threaten me with being locked up in the town police cell whenever she caught me scaling her backyard wall to retrieve my football – which happened a lot. This was because she was the only person in the street to lock and bolt her backyard gate – something that caused a great deal of suspicion in the neighbourhood.

Such 'unfriendly' behaviour eventually caused a major row in the street between Fadge and another neighbour, Bella Smith, who was one of the most popular people locally. We all liked Bella in our house – she was seen as the Good Samaritan of the neighbourhood, because whenever anyone needed advice or was in poor health, it was to Bella they turned, any time of the day or night. She was also the street's unofficial mid-wife and had watched most of us grow up from the day we were born. So an argument that involved Bella was astonishing.

The 'snowdrift incident' – as it was later called – happened in front of most of the neighbours during what was one of the harshest winters we had ever had. Unlike some, my pals and I loved the huge snowfall, and we often had major snowball fights in the street. On this particular morning, some of my pals – who shall remain nameless – had piled a large mound of snow against Fadge's backyard door, which she then struggled to open later that morning. She eventually emerged, red-faced and panting, only to spot Bella on the street, innocently brushing her backyard steps of snow. Stomping over to her, Fadge immediately accused Bella of blocking her gate, waving her fist in the air. Under attack by her hostile neighbour, Bella defended herself, but Fadge refused to listen. The row grew until Bella withdrew and reappeared, armed with her trusty frying pan, while Fadge had disappeared into her own house and emerged with a sturdy walking stick.

To the astonishment of the crowd that had by now gathered, attracted by the rising shrieks, there then followed much wild flourishings and swishings of weapons. Suddenly, the local vicar, Reverend Duncan, appeared on his Monday morning clergy rounds, carefully walking down the icy street. He approached the two warriors – bravely, I thought – and, after a few minutes, he and the Bible he was flourishing had persuaded them to cease battle. Much to my disappointment, not one spot of blood had been shed. The two women withdrew without a handshake, and this surprised me, for my dad had always told me that fighters (boxers) always shook hands after a fight. Perhaps, I thought, it only applied to men?

*   *   *

One late afternoon I was enjoying a fishing expedition at Stoney's pond, a small, shallow stretch of water at the top of the large meadow next to the edge of Stella Woods. Despite the fact that no stream flowed into it, the pond was never stagnant. My uncle Billy had once told me that its source was in Australia, and this fact was confirmed when Alan Dodds claimed he had seen a partially submerged crocodile lurking amongst the reeds and bulrushes! From then on, Stoney's pond was a very exciting and dangerous place to fish!

Keeping my eyes peeled for reptiles, I was just landing my third stickleback when the mournful sound of the town's air-raid klaxon belted forth across the valley. I immediately picked up my jam-jar catch and set off for home and safety. However, on the way back I was caught by the sight of two majestic swans in flight whirring their way home to reedy pastures. At the same time I saw in the sky, much higher up, the strange formation of thin, wispy, white lines of cloud zig-zagging through the sky, often forming figure-of-eight patterns overhead; interwoven with occasional puffs of darker smoke. An air fight was in progress! I was captivated. I could see and hear formations of droning, large, dark planes in the sky, and buzzing around them, with their bright fuselages glinting in the sun, were what I guessed were our own fighter aircraft.

The continuous wail of the town siren reminded me that I should be off home and closeted with my family in our Mary Street air-raid shelter. So, despite the amazing aerial l theatre above, I ran towards home, careful not to spill my jam-jar's contents.

Later that evening, sitting with my parents listening to the Rediffusion radio news broadcast, I heard that there had been a massive aerial dogfight over the River Tyne. Several Spitfire fighter aircraft had sent a huge squadron of German Junker bombers packing. Hurrah! We were winning the war! We all then stood up to attention as the national anthem then played on the radio. That night, tucked in my bed, another ambition began to form in my mind – I wanted to be a Spitfire pilot!

The next evening the dreaded *Luftwaffe* returned under the sneaky cover of darkness and heavy rain clouds. I was rudely awakened by the wailing siren and, just as my mam was shaking me to get dressed quickly, there were two tremendous explosive 'clumps'. My dad, who had been standing at the open window whilst dressing, suddenly flew across the bedroom – like Peter Pan – and landed in a heap on the bed, where only two minutes before he had been in a deep slumber. Seemingly unshaken, he got up muttering, 'Whey, thet was a closin!' and, with my sister and mam in tow, swept me up in his arms to join the stream of our neighbours, who were heading for the outside air-raid shelter at the top of the street.

In the cold, dank, reinforced building, containing row upon row of wood slatted bunks, Bella Smith was already there before us, handing out hot tea from a large Thermos flask and extra blankets, all the while humming, 'We're gann te hang oot the weshing on the Seigefield line'. Soon everyone joined in for the chorus, determined not to be upset. Suddenly, bursting through the entrance of the shelter, my aunty

Olive appeared carrying my cousin Edmund, and she was soon followed by my uncle. They were visibly shaking and their faces were covered in soot. 'We've bin bombed – we've bin bloody bombed!' my aunty exclaimed and was immediately comforted by my mam and the other women in the shelter.

Now that the family had reached the safety of the shelter, they soon settled onto one of the bunks, and apart from their black faces, they appeared unharmed. After a short while, Aunty Olive even managed to have a laugh at the situation – standing up, covered in soot, with only the whites of her eyes visible and with her hands in the air, she started to sing the opening line to Irving Berlin's 'Mammy', which had been famously sung by Al Johnson. In doing so, she immediately released the pent-up tension in the bunker, and this despite the occasional, explosive 'clump' continuing outside.

The next day I set off to search for war trophies – pieces of bomb and other shrapnel – but despite scouring the streets for ages around Delacour Road (where a bomb had demolished two houses and killed four people), I returned home with only a collection of rusty nails, a horseshoe and pieces of old metal guttering to show for all my efforts (the result, I believed, of the cunning Germans filling their bombs with scrap ammunition). However, when I eventually arrived home, I saw a magnificent piece of shrapnel sitting in the corner of my very own backyard! Don Craven, a slightly older pal who lived on Delacour Road (about half a mile from Mary Street) had brought it round to show me.

The previous evening, he and his family had sat out the air raid in their own Anderson shelter (a small, reinforced, metal shelter which people could build for themselves in their own back gardens). The piece of shrapnel he had brought round had come from his neighbour's garden – a near miss for Don. He claimed that he had also found a small piece of one of his unfortunate neighbours hanging in the hedge at the back of his garden, and offered to show it to me and my pals for a penny a glance. Fascinated, we all agreed, but it only turned out to be a discarded chicken leg his parents had feasted on the evening before – he had tied a small bandage around it and covered it in tomato sauce! Needless to say we got our money back!

Although the air raids caused a lot of upheaval, I continued to enjoy my own free-roaming and happy life. Even at primary school, we welcomed the disruption of classes that the air-raid siren signaled. Once the klaxon screeched through the air, we would all tidy up our desks, and then line up single file to troop out of the classroom towards the cloakroom. Pulling on our coats, we would loop the string-tied brown box containing our gas masks around our necks, and then off we would go to the school's air-raid shelters.

Alan Redpath was the tallest boy in the school, and he always donned his gas mask on the way to the shelters, saying that as he was head and shoulders taller than anyone else, he would be the first to be attacked by the aerial-delivered, Nazi poison gas! (This, we found out, was because he had spotted such a danger a few weeks previously in the film *Dive Bombers*, which had been showing at the Empire cinema.)

As we made our way to the shelters, we would carry out our rehearsed regimented march through the play yard, up some steep concrete steps and into a field, where, one by one we would enter the dark, musty, concrete air-raid shelters. Once we were settled on the wood-slatted benches, our teacher, Miss Cameron, would offer each of us a single delicious Horlicks tablet, often the only sweets we had tasted since the previous air raid. A free sweet was no small thing, and so we often all cheered when we heard the warning sound of the siren!

One evening, my sister and I were up late, having been allowed to listen along with our parents to a spooky radio drama series, featuring Valentine Dyal as 'The Man in Black'. Joan was lying on the settee with two cushions held to her ears, and I was curled up safe in my mam's lap, when there was a break in the transmission and a news announcer came on apologising for the interruption (which I was quite happy with, as the heroine was about to confront the bloodthirsty villain). The news announcer then said that reports had just come in that enemy bombers were dropping a new bomb cunningly disguised as children's toys or brightly coloured packages, designed to lure the unwary into picking up the lethal items. These bombs contained enough explosives to kill or seriously maim the innocent victim. After this announcement, the rest of the radio drama carried on, but not before Dad told us how important it was to be vigilant and to not pick up any suspicious objects whilst we were on our travels around the area.

The next day after school, my pals and I (apart from Brave Buffalo) all met at Summerhill for our traditional pow-wow and the newly added ritual of the smoking of a pipe of peace (an old discarded clay pipe, which we filled with cinnamon sticks when we had them and imaginary ones when we didn't). After a short game of 'Cowp-yer-creels' (leapfrog), a breathless Brave Buffalo suddenly arrived, flinging himself onto the grass and exclaiming, 'Ave just foound one of those Jerman boms that me ma towld me aboot, lying under a gorze bush!' Then he leapt to his feet and, spanking his backside as if was riding his palomino, shouted. 'Follow me lads!' and sprinted off down the grassy bank towards Stella Woods.

Sure enough, when we all got to the 'target area', Brave Buffalo, indicating the need for total silence, pointed out a sinister-looking white carton with its lid intact, lying underneath a large gorse bush. We all immediately backed away, Running Brave disappearing in a cloud of dust! Crazy Hands (Billie Hutchinson) whispered that the bomb was probably sensitive to noise and an immediate hush enveloped us. Brave Buffalo, then pointing in Apache sign-language, beckoned for us to retreat and we slowly withdrew from the ticking bomb, Crazy Hands having said that he was sure he had heard some ticking from inside the box. Although the rest of us had not heard any ticking noise from the bomb, we voted three-to-one against Brave Buffalo's suggestion to blow the bomb up from a distance with some large stones that were lying on the banks of the nearby stream.

After some more bickering, we finally agreed to sprint home and tell our mams of our dangerous find! Our discovery soon swept through the town like wildfire. The local town constable was informed and he in turn alerted the fire brigade, who then in turn contacted the local Home Guard sergeant. The road to Summerhill was closed and within an hour a bomb-disposal team had arrived on the scene.

Brave Buffalo (who was by now being heralded as a hero!) went with his dad to guide the military and security teams to the danger area, before retreating back to safety on the summit of Summerhill, where we had all gathered to watch the exciting event. Snotty Biggins decided to take no chances and blocked his fingers into his ears! After twenty minutes or so, we saw the tin-helmeted, khaki-dressed soldiers run from the edge of the woods and take cover behind a large mound in the field a few hundred yards below us. Then an officer came striding out of the woods and waved to his fellow soldiers to approach. Everyone then started to clap and cheer the brave soldiers in relief as we realised all was safe, although we were somewhat disappointed that the huge explosion we had expected had not happened. It was with some difficulty that we were able to prise Snotty Biggins's fingers from his ears to tell him that it was over, and with our jeers of 'Softy! Softy!' ringing in his unblocked ears he ran off down the path to be comforted (yet again) by his mam!

Back in town, Brave Buffalo was the centre of attention and basked in his glory. Perhaps the white carton had cunningly concealed a massive bomb and BB had saved the town from destruction? It was several days later that my uncle Billy, who was a part-time fireman, told my mam that the dangerous, German carton bomb had contained nothing more than a pair of worn-out sandshoes! However the authorities had decided not to announce the real contents of the package as they wished to keep the public on high alert. This, of course, was a lucky decision for Brave Buffalo, who feasted on his hero status for many months to come!

*   *   *

Like my friends, most of my free time was spent playing in and around the woods at Stella. There I would find the wild aniseed-tasting fennel, and one particular, friendly, old oak tree that bore my initials carved into its base. My favourite spot in the whole area was my secret den, which nestled beneath a huge hazel tree, which I christened 'Goliath', and which I often sought out for its advice. If the leaves rustled immediately in response to my question, then I knew I had it's approval. On the other hand, if the tree's foliage remained motionless at the exact end of my question, then I knew this meant a 'no' to my query. Sometimes I would cheat, so that when, such as, I got a 'no' answer to my question – 'Was I going to become a millionaire?' – I would wait for some time in the hope that a breeze would arrive to give me my desired answer!

Goliath was surrounded by tall masses of ferns and, as the sole tenant of my den, I also had the bonus of my own magnificent carpet of bluebells, which in springtime surrounded me as far as the eye could see. My den boasted two comfortable, mossy log seats and a three-walled framework of latticed hawthorn branches, which I had expertly slotted together. My secret hiding place was also next to the fast-flowing stream that ran down the centre of the woods.

Often, to get to my den, I would do an exhausting, non-stop sprint, zigzagging through the trees from nearby Path Head Mill, imagining that I had escaped from hostile, well-armed Nazi guards. I would go leaping and bounding through the woods, sidestepping the evil bramble patches riddled with land mines and avoiding the cunning and painful nettle beds, which hid vicious, razor-sharp trip wires. Arriving breathless at my HQ, I would squat on the mossy grass and dangle my bare feet in the ice-cold current of the stream. Then, lying back on my mattress of sweet-smelling foliage I would gaze upwards through Goliath's sun-dappled leaves and listen to the rippling of the stream as it slid over the large stepping stones I had placed there, to allow a quick escape from German paratroopers. Here, also, I could suck the delightful aniseed juice from a nearby growing stalk of wild fennel or think about that morning's discovery of a wren's nest containing seven tiny, red-spotted eggs. In such a place I was content; the war just one small part of my happy world.

Chapter Five

Santa Who?

It hit us like a bombshell! Dickie Biggins was the bearer of this astonishing news and, being in exile from the Mary Street gang (because of his constant snitching on us to our parents), his outburst initially stunned us. It was just a few days before Christmas Eve and I was happily thinking about the contents of Santa Claus's bulging sack destined for number 27 Mary Street. I had never once questioned Santa's ability to carry tons of toys and deliver them down the thousands of chimneys across the many towns and villages on the night before Christmas.

No doubt Dickie Biggins (or 'Yellow Snot' as we Apaches often called him, as he always had a runny nose) wanted to get his own back on us after being continually shunned by the gang. His shocking news came during our weekly pow-wow on the summit of

Summerhill, after he had singly failed to get back into our good graces with an offer of some liquorice sticks and a free bite of his eater (ripe apple). Treating such an offer with suitable scorn, we all resumed talking about the toys we wanted for Christmas, expecting Yellow Snot to leave us and go home.

Nearly in tears, Dickie shouted as he left the reservation: 'Anyhoo, thors nee such thing as Santa Claus; aks yer mam!' before running off. Despite our immediate disbelief, Dickie had unfortunately sown a seed of doubt in my own mind, though I scoffed along with the others at his stupid suggestion. We pledged our total confidence and allegiance to the white-bearded Father Christmas and rejected Yellow Snot's selfish foolishness.

Although our country had been at war for over three years, I had been able to carry on with my everyday fun and adventures without being over affected by it all. I had assumed that this coming Christmas would follow the same pattern as all the other ones, but now I had this nagging doubt about the identity of Santa Claus.

The week before Christmas had started off with everyone in the street in a jolly, festive mood, and as a young eight-year-old I was hugely excited about the ever closer Christmas Day and the generosity of Santa Claus. My mam had said that provided I was in bed and fast asleep early on Christmas Eve, she would follow the traditional custom of leaving a small plate of mince pies by the fireplace for Santa to eat in order to sustain him on his long journey back to Lapland in the frozen North.

Wandering up Mary Street, I loved to look into our neighbours' front-parlour windows, each showing multi-coloured paper decorations hanging across the ceiling, all carefully avoiding the single gas mantles. Many windows showed small Christmas trees draped with streamers, silver tinsel and numerous coloured shining globes. These enthralling decorations often reflected the flames of the roaring coal fires burning merrily away in the fireplaces, and they often swung in tandem whenever the front or back doors were opened just for a second, allowing the persistent chilly north-east gusts to sneak into the homes.

Indeed, 'Shut that bloody door!' was often heard throughout the street as the snow fell gently, blanketing and transforming the town. This handily meant that there would be no need to send any Christmas cards, I thought; something Dad had said was unnecessary when there, outside, before our very eyes, was the perfect real Christmas card. He would add, "Why go to the trouble and cost of sending a card reflecting the time of year, when we could all wish each other a Merry Christmas face-to-face?" Getting into his stride, my dad would continue that there was no need to invest in cards and stamps to give our neighbours a seasonal message when they only lived next door! Anyway, Dad argued, Christmas cards were for the posh people of the town, who had money to burn. Mam often called him a scrooge after this rant, but in truth I agreed with Dad, as very few Christmas cards were sent in our working-class area, and I couldn't remember us ever having received one.

Anyway, fresh from Yellow Snot's shocking news about Santa, I decided to confront my mam about the upcoming visit of Santa Claus (to get the necessary reassurance about the seasonal presents destined for me that year). My sister Joan was washing up plates and cutlery in the scullery sink, but Mam was nowhere to be seen. 'Your mam's next door,' she replied when I asked her where she was. Perhaps, I thought, my sister, older than me by three years, could surely confirm that Yellow Snot was having us on?

Joan was obviously in a hurry to finish her chores and tut-tutted when I casually asked if she was expecting anything special this Christmas from Santa Claus. 'Don't be daft!' she exclaimed. 'Don't you know that he doesn't exist?!' and with that she finished off the last plate and headed for the front room. Stunned, I chased after her and demanded she confirm his non-existence once more and that all our Christmas presents were therefore from our parents. No Santa Claus! I was still reeling from the shock. Yellow Snot had been right all the time!

This news had come as a massive blow for me – not only had the magical spirit of Christmas that I had held so dear been destroyed in just a few seconds, but worse still, my mam (whom I had believed in everything she told me) had lied to me! Why, only last year, I thought darkly, Joan and I had crept downstairs silently in the dark of night just to check that Santa had not forgotten to pay us a visit. Sure enough the evidence of his night-time visit had been there, with several boxes and well-wrapped parcels stacked in the parlour.

These presents were never in the traditional, seasonally decorated wrapping paper – as my dad would remark, 'Thet's for the posh folk with money to burn!' – but instead they were covered in the brown paper Mam had saved throughout the year from the Co-operative Society's weekly delivered, brown-paper-wrapped grocery parcels. The presents were always neatly stacked up in two separate piles on the settee, with the traditional, festive stockings (my dad's grey woollen socks) hanging from the mantelpiece, at each corner of the black, lead fire range. Each stocking held similar gifts – six walnuts, a tangerine, some Dainty Dinah toffees and two apples. My stocking also held a small box of liggies (marbles), whilst my sister's contained a pencil set.

My sister (whom I now realised must have been carrying out a false charade for some time) had convinced me of Santa's visit to our house by pointing out evidence showing he had been there – two, large boot prints in the cooled white ashes in the fire grate (showing his recent chimney entrance) and crumbs from the mince pies which were all that was left of the treat we had set out for him the night before (a sure sign, I had thought, that Santa had paid his seasonal visit). So, I was at a complete loss to explain this baffling on-going deception over the past few years!

Just then Mam entered the room and I immediately wailed, 'No Santa Claus! Why have you been lying to me all this time?', sobbing with real disappointment. Mam took me in her arms, giving me a tight squeeze and a cuddle, and explained that she realised that it was difficult for me to understand, but very similar to fairies, goblins and Peter Pan, Santa Claus only existed for very young children in order to capture their imagination and to learn from these fairy-tales. Now that I was nearly grown up, it was time for me not to need these fables. 'Whey,' she said to me, 'aren't ye noo one of the tallest lads in the street? An' also one of the canniest footballers! Noo yer growing up fast you'll soon be a man, so it's best ye kna aboot these things noo!' and with that she gave my sister a withering look. My mam then gave me a piece of Holland toffee to stifle my wailing. My tears began to subside and feeling that I must have grown a further six inches I accepted another toffee.

Then I scampered out of the house to discover how many of the rest of the Mary Street gang had been told that Santa Claus was just for young children. I called on each Apache Brave, one by one, and arranged for a pow-wow to discuss this shocking topic for the next day. I was the first to arrive at our reservation and soon the remainder of the gang ran towards me whooping and chanting in true Apache-style. As was our custom, once we were all together we all greeted each other with our right arms across our chests, followed by 'How!' We then immediately started talking about why we were there, and on the subject of Father Christmas, each member of the gang spoke:

Running Brave (sheepishly): 'Ave nown since last Xmas, cause me dad towled me thet Santa

Claus had bin shot doon by a Gorman Meshersmit on his way doon from Iceland, but Aaah had te keep it te mesell'!'

Crazy Hands (crestfallen): 'Wey ave known aall the time. Anyway since last year, aah seen me dad in middle of the neet, creep into wor room and put the presents himsell' at the bottom of wor bed.'

Chief Brown Legs (blushing): 'Ave niver believed in Santa Claus anyhow, 'cause aah niver got what aah wanted – a model clockwork railway set with real lines and the Flying Scotsman. Aal I got was clowes and bukes!'

And finally Brave Buffalo (brazenly): 'Ave nown fer sumtime noo. Me granny towld me that Santa Claus was gittin' hard up and had gone oot of busness. So any presents were from me mam and dad, if they could afford it! Last yeer aal aah got wore sum nuts and marbles in me stocking and half a box of dates. Me stocking had a hole in it and aah lost the other half of the dates to me greedy brothers!'

I was now fully aware of the drift of the meeting and summed up the pow-wow with the fib (never a lie, cross your heart and hope to die) that I, too, had been fully aware of the non-existence of the silly Santa Claus and, somewhat blushing, joined in with agreeing with the rest of the gang, who I now realised all 'spoke with forked tongues'!

Chapter Six

The Salesman

I had always been a bright, confident boy. I never felt at all awkward with my pals or the adults around me. My confidence grew enormously, however, once my dad had bought me some boxing gloves and taught me to fight in self-defence. The respect of my pals grew along with my ability to use a straight left – a step above the slapping, pawing and pushing we had previously used in a fight!

These newly-learned skills were to prove very important, because soon after I caught the eye of the infamous 'enemy school' bully, Cameron McGinty. Known as 'Camma', he was of a similar age to me and went to the local Catholic school, which was on the left-hand side of the steeply inclined Blaydon Bank road, directly opposite my own Protestant school, Blaydon Primary. Unfortunately my journey home after school took me across the main road, so I could go up the steep flight of steps to the higher street level, and this meant I also had to run the gauntlet of passing the entrance to St Joseph's Catholic school.

This school had always been the enemy school of Blaydon Primary for as long as I could remember. However, I was totally ignorant as to why there was a war going on between the two schools. The regular exchange of oaths, scuffles, stone-throwing and even fierce snowball fights added to the intense dislike the rival pupils had for one another, pitting Protestant against Catholic and Catholic against Protestant on a daily basis. Although I knew I was 'Church of England' and belonged to St Cuthbert's church choir, I could not see why we were supposed to hate Catholics. Surely, I reasoned, we worshipped the same God?

I once overheard my aunty Betty, talking about this with her neighbour Mrs Brown, when I was calling for my cousin to play football in the street. Both women were keen members of St Cuthbert's, and especially of the St Cuthbert's Mothers' Union, and they always spoke out against any religious practices that were not C of E.

In between her slurps of hot, strong tea, Mrs B sat in my aunty's kitchen and said how disgraceful it was that Papist followers of God were forced to pay for the use of their pew seats and had to confess all their sins, and yet were then allowed to get away Scot free with a life of crime and sin without punishment! Overhearing such comments only made me more puzzled. There was only one thing I was sure of – we hated the Catholics and the Catholics hated us. For me, this meant it was best to avoid them altogether, especially Camma, who had built a fierce reputation in the area as a formidable opponent and a bully.

Often, while playing in the wooded Dene near our house, word would reach us that the dreaded Camma and his renegades were coming – he would always announce his presence with a wild Commanche war cry, and on hearing this bloodcurdling shriek, we would flee, terrified, to the safety of our homes. Camma was slight of build and came from the oldest part of town, near the banks of the River Tyne, which was often seen as one of the poorest areas of Blaydon. (Indeed, the people who lived farther up the slopes of the town saw themselves as better than the 'down-streeters' – as they called them – because not only did they have their own separate backyard 'lavvies' (toilets), but they also had the luxury of a washbasin inside the house as well!)

Camma came from a large, Catholic down-streeter family. His parents had a reputation for quarrelling violently with their neighbours and everyone knew their children were wild and unruly. Camma himself was very rough and aggressive, particularly towards non-Catholics, and he would often challenge anyone who came across his path to a fight. He even challenged the bigger boys to battle, and because of his ugly face and mass of wild ginger hair, his opponents would quickly duck his aggressive taunts; which only added to his reputation as a bully.

This, then, was the one person I prayed to avoid on my way home from school. So it was with a sinking heart that I heard, one Friday afternoon as I arrived at the top of my street, someone running behind me shouting, 'Proti dog! Proti dog!' Spinning around, and before I could escape down the lane to the safety of number 27, I found myself face-to-face with the formidable Camma and one of his Catholic cronies, Jack Appleyard. Grasping my shoulders, Camma pushed me roughly against the wall, and growled, 'See that fist? It's ganna smash yer nose to bits. See that fist?' – pointing to his left hand – 'It's ganna reely buggaup yer mooth and when aas finished am ganna googe yer eyes oot!'

I was terrified. My heart was pounding. Flashing through my mind was the thought that death was reaching for me, either that or I was soon due for a painful visit to Doctor Morrison. I was firmly held in a vice-like grip by my assassin and being shaken like a rabbit. In a panic I looked down the lane towards my home, when suddenly a miracle happened! Mam's head popped out of the backyard gate, looking up the road towards us. Seeing salvation close at hand, I was able to twist suddenly and, without a word, take my evil opponent by complete surprise, hammering a straight left jab right into his face with all the force I could muster.

The look of horror and astonishment on Camma's face was a joy to behold as he released his grip and fell to the pavement squealing in agony. His crony looked just as shocked and yelled, 'Yer didn't 'ave to dee that!' before hauling up his defeated friend to retreat, whose nose and cheek were streaming blood onto his shirt. When I arrived at my house, Mam cheered and clapped my bravery, and produced an extra potted-meat sandwich and two slices of granny loaf for my tea.

Some days later, I was walking past St Joseph's Catholic school and saw Camma and his crony coming towards me. I felt nervous, wondering whether Camma was out for revenge. As they neared me I held my breath, but Camma and his friend both walked sheepishly past me with their heads down. I let my breath out explosively once they had gone past. The boxing lessons had paid off!

My confidence grew with this triumph now that I knew I could take care of myself. The news of my defeat of Camma soon spread all over school and I gained the respect of all my fellow schoolchildren. I felt older, ready to face the future, confident that one day I could be whatever I chose to be – a steam-engine driver, a Spitfire pilot or even, now, a professional boxer. Of course, all these would be cover activities to mask my true calling – that of International Courier Spy!

Still, as the autumn passed, I fell back into my regular pastimes of haunting Stella Woods and hiding out in my den. Looking down our street towards the river, I could see that the day's chilly north-east wind was creating small, white-crested waves across the surface of the dark, coaly waters of the Tyne, and I knew that winter was not far away. I was on my way to Rogers, the hardware shop, for a clothes-line for my mam, because I had snapped our washing-line when playing tug-of-war with it with my pals in Tweddle's field the day before (much to the fury of my mam and gran who shared the line every Monday washday).

I soon reached the shop and it wasn't long before I was at the front of the queue. Whilst I had been waiting, I had noticed in the corner of the store a large, well-stacked pile of firewood logs, with a sign saying: 'Winter is nigh! Buy now whilst stocks last! Only 1/3d per sack!' The logs seemed to be the same as the firewood I had chopped for my gran the day before in a nearby spinney (before my ill-fated game of tug-of-war) and where I remembered there were still many large, fallen branches and trees that had been blown down by the violent storm that had happened last winter. I soon replaced my mam's washing-line, but my mind was now full of a plan inspired by the logs I had seen.

The next morning – being a Saturday – I took my two younger cousins Edmund and Freddie, along with a 'bogey' (wheeled cart) that my dad had made from an old pram, off to the spinney. My cousins were important to my plan working – although I was quite willing to help run errands at home, any other hard work I tried to avoid, and unfortunately my plan involved lots of hard work; though luckily, for me, this was something I planned on Edmund and Freddie doing (not that they liked to do hard work either).

I knew that both Edmund and Freddie were keen rivals when it came to games or races. So, on arrival at the spinney, I suggested that they should be the first ever contestants of a newly introduced Olympic event: the Wood Log Marathon. The winner, I said, would be the 'athlete' who chopped the most logs over the next hour and, as a prize, he would get two sips from my fizzy Tizer bottle and half of my large cooking apple, plus, of course, the Olympic title. My younger cousins readily agreed and, on the word 'Go!', raced over to the fallen trees and branches with their home-borrowed axes. They responded to my shouts of encouragement and my running commentary on their progress – 'And now it's Freddie just ahead, but here comes Edmund with a magnificent log and he may well have overtaken his rival! No! For here comes Freddie with two well-cut logs and he's now the overall leader!' – by increasing their efforts. Straining and sweating heavily, they quickly built two separate piles of wood, while I sat on a nearby log, sipping my bottle of Tizer and enjoying my role as a sports commentator!

Eventually, my two exhausted cousins slumped to the ground, having piled up two large stacks of logs. I congratulated both contestants and decided that the event had ended in a well-earned tie, and gave both winners one half each of my green apple and a share of the remainder of the Tizer. Then I loaded the logs onto the bogey (both cousins by now being too worn out!) and, bidding them farewell, set off for Rogers, the hardware store.

On entering the shop, I found to my delight that the store was empty of customers. I wanted to talk to Mr Rogers, and an audience would have put me off. I already knew the shop owner, because like many tradesmen in the town Mr Rogers sang in the same church choir as me and of course I had shopped in his store many times before. He was a short, jolly man, who lived in a lakeside detached house in the posh area of Blaydon called Axwell Park. He always seemed to talk – and at church, sing – out of the corner of his mouth, and he was a wonderful whistler. In the choir he sang with real passion from the choir stalls and, despite his difficulty in reaching the top tenor notes, he was a favourite of the choirmaster, Mr Lawton (though he was never trusted with a musical solo!).

Mr Rogers wore a clean, white apron in the shop, unlike his assistant Peggy, who had a miserable face, lank hair and always seemed to wear a dirty apron stained with oil and streaks of paint. Her 'hackey' (filthy) appearance was due to the fact that Mr Rogers only took customers' orders and handled the money, leaving Peggy to do everything else.

So, wheeling in my trolley, I asked Mr R if he would like to buy my fresh load of logs (my plan being that he would buy them all instantly and I would have a welcome extra bit of money). Mr Rogers looked the logs over, lifting a couple from the cart and sniffing the aromatic pine smell. I nervously waited for his reply. Eventually he smiled and nodding happily he asked me how much I wanted for them.

I was both delighted and yet at the same stumped (as they say in the timber trade). Whilst I had already ventured into sales with some blackberries I had harvested the previous year[1], I was still new to the selling game and I had not thought of a price. Remembering how much Mr Rogers' logs were selling for, I suggested what I thought would be a reasonable price and held my breath. After a pause, Mr R agreed. Success! I left the shop with four shillings jingling

[1] See *Soapy Business* by John Solomon

in my pocket – in one go I had nearly as much as four weeks' pocket money! I ran all the way home to celebrate my good fortune and to break the news to my mam. Already I was turning my mind to what I could sell next. This sales game seemed to be easy!

Chapter Seven

The Picture Hoose!

Blaydon not only had various shops and pubs, it also boasted five fish-and-chip shops and three cinemas – four if you included the Rex cinema a couple of miles away at the top of Blaydon Bank, in the small village of Winlaton. The status or pecking order in the town for the three cinemas – or 'picture hooses' as the locals called them – placed the Plaza as the top cinema. The Plaza had a seating area that was divided in two: the upstairs 'balcony' catered for the posh members of the town, whilst everyone else sat in the cheaper (and therefore more popular) stalls below.

Of the three cinemas, the Plaza could seat the most people, and its seating was all the same, being cushioned throughout in a deep, velvety red fabric. The inside of the cinema was always clean, and the rear of each seat even had its own ashtray attached.

Seconds after the programme interval began at the Plaza, a spotlight and piped music would announce the arrival of two tray-carrying attendants selling ice cream, when it was available, who stood at each corner of the screen. These young women relished their fleeting, film star fanfare introduction to the audience, and dressed in their smart cream uniform and matching pillbox hats, would proudly walk down the aisle to the front of the cinema. With each step, they would sway their hips and make 'K-legs' (this a family joke on the shape the girls' legs made as they walked along trying to bear up the heavy weight of their trays whilst tottering on high heels). Once they had reached the screen they would take up their stations and, with a dramatic sweep of the arm, they would point a finger to their trays. Each girl also wore lots of lipstick, and their 'buy me' smiles meant that a lot of men would gather round them in the interval.

Because of this, lots of young women wanted to be one of the Plaza's ice-cream attendants. My sister said that these girls were never without many offers of courtship. Still I found it all annoying, because the men always got in the way of an honest chap trying to buy an ice choc bar!

At the Plaza you had to be on your best behaviour, because the no-nonsense manager immediately ejected anyone making any noise during the showing of the film. Not that anyone complained at this, because the booting out of such a person was often met with a loud round of applause from the audience!

The next cinema down from the Plaza was the Pavilion, or 'the Hall' as it was locally known. The Pavilion Theatre sat at the bottom of Mary Street and was part of the large Co-op building, which also housed a bakery among other things. This 'number two' cinema was privately owned by a Mr Smolt, a huge man always smartly dressed in a pinstriped suit and a dark Homburg hat. According to Mrs Richardson, who lived in our street and who worked at the Pavilion as a part-time cleaner, Mr Smolt had had an unfortunate accident whilst driving his car (after over-indulging at the celebrations of a Masonic Lodge meeting), and had knocked down and killed two people. At his trial, he had gotten off with a token fine, a short driving ban and a severe warning from the judge, who happened to be a fellow Lodge member.

Afterwards, I would sometimes see him arrive at his cinema at the bottom of our street in a large, black, chauffer-driven Austin Princess limousine. He would stagger out of the car and go into the cinema building, only to reappear a few minutes later with a large leather bag – the evening's takings – which he would carry off having been poured back into the car by his chauffeur. Mr Smolt obviously continued drinking, but after the accident many people took to avoiding him (except for his Masonic friends) and so despite its varied film programmes, for a long time the Pavilion had a hard time matching the popularity of the Plaza cinema.

The Empire theatre was something else! The first cinema built in Blaydon, the 'Empire Electric Theatre' was so old it had once shown silent movies. It had a split-seating area, with an entrance fee of only 6d for the stalls and 9d for the balcony. However, the 'Lop' (as it was often called) was a dowdy, run-down, smelly place, and its programmes were often main feature films mixed with 'B'-starred pictures, featuring unknown actors struggling with boring plots. It could certainly never match the quality of the feature films at the Plaza, and its audience not only had to put up with the strong smells of Domestos and Dettol, but they were also forced to sit on uncomfortable, hard wooden benches at the front of the stalls or patched-up, spring-twanging, musty fabric-covered seats at the rear of the stalls and in the balcony.

Also, the film-projector at the Empire was on the ground-floor level, so that any latecomers over six-foot tall would be greeted with a chorus of hisses and boos as their shadowy image covered up Errol Flynn's sword attack on the Sheriff of Nottingham! Yet despite this, the Empire had a strong following of loyal filmgoers who were not willing to pay the higher entrance fees at the Plaza.

However, whenever I could afford it, I preferred to go to the Plaza cinema. At every evening performance the manager, Mr Tindall (who had a bright, red face; slicked-down, brilliantined, ginger hair and a waxed moustache), would personally welcome his adult customers. Saturday evenings were the most popular showings – the 'Full' notices often displayed well before the start of the programme – and Mr Tindall's wife (of Dorothy Lamour fame) often turned up on those evenings.

Mr Tindall was of military bearing and was always dressed in a smart tuxedo. He had a cheesy smile and would greet every adult with 'Good to see you, sir!' before ushering them through the pastel green, rococo-tiled entrance hall towards the ticket kiosk, where they were greeted by the elder sister of Billy Drury (who was on the choir with me). We christened Billy's sister Olive Oyl because she was the spitting image of the wife of our great cartoon hero Popeye! The good thing about Olive Oyl was that if I was able to go to the cinema with Billy in tow, she would gave us free entry tickets for the posh upstairs 1/9d seats, where we would sit surrounded by the town's VIPs and their families, like Doctor Morrison, Police Sergeant Armstrong and Mr Clough, my school headmaster.

Normally, however, I sat in the 6d stalls with my Mary Street pals and we would sit spellbound during the Saturday morning children's matinees, where we were allowed to scream, shout and sing our way through the adventures of Flash Gordon and Hopalong Cassidy. I much preferred this to the weekly evening performances, where I would cringe whenever there were any kissing scenes by the Hollywood stars. Luckily the Saturday morning matinees rarely had any such 'clarty' (slushy) scenes and I was free to enjoy the parade of pistols, rifles and tomahawks as the 'baduns', rustlers, bank robbers and town bullies were defeated, usually by them being thrown out of a saloon-bar window. My pals and I agreed that the only 'clarty kissy' scenes which were all right were the ones which involved a token peck on the cheek from the 'school marm' to Hopalong Cassidy for rescuing her and her pupils from the mighty Cochise and his painted renegades.

Apart from the Saturday matinees, the other thing my pals and I looked forward to was the weekly Pathé news bulletin, introduced by the picture of a crowing white cockerel. Although most of the news items bored us, when it came to the reporting of the current war situation we all paid attention. The film shots of the disciplined German army marching in tandem with their pompous high goose step caused us all to laugh and feel sure we would win the problem in gaining victory over an enemy who couldn't walk properly and wore helmets shaped like chamber pots!

However, as soon as the image of Herr Hitler appeared on the screen, the whole audience would start booing and then shout a well-rehearsed chorus of 'Hadaway Hitler! Hadaway Hitler! Hadaway doon te hell!', repeated over and over until Adolf faded from the screen.

On our Saturday morning matinee visits, a regular feature of our time there would be that Brave Buffalo (Philip Lynn) would always have to leave his seat to go to the toilets before the main film began. On one particular morning, feeling the urge to go as well as I was filled up with Tizer, I decided a few seconds later to join him. Just as I pushed open the toilet door, which was next to the emergency exit, I was astonished to find the washroom packed with several lads, most of whom were Brave Buffalo's younger brothers and also one or two other lads I recognised from our class at school. Suddenly, to my surprise, a pair of legs appeared through the open top half of the toilet window, which looked out onto the street.

I later found out that these intruders had each paid Philip one penny (as opposed to the normal entry admission of 6d) as a 'reward' for releasing the inside catch of the toilet window and then acting as a lookout man for them in order to allow each of his 'guests' to slip unnoticed into the darkened cinema hall. Brave Buffalo saw this covert operation as a challenge similar to the recent film we had seen involving a daring escape of prisoners of war – except that his controlled operation was in reverse!

The next weekend at our traditional Summerhill pow-wow, after the ceremonial passing of the cinnamon pipe of peace had been done, we eventually decided not to tell our parents about Brave Buffalo's cunning Plaza scheme. Though we were uncomfortable with his actions, we had also vowed never to tell on any member of the tribe. Of course, Brave Buffalo's promise that he would give us part of his takings didn't hurt either!

One of our favourite films that we went to see was a terrific wartime movie, which showed the battle adventures and courage of a small group of outnumbered British soldier holed up in a sniper's nest, bravely fighting a Nazi SS platoon who, unlike the Tommys, were supported by a massive armoured tank. It was just getting towards the end of the film, and tough British hero Sergeant 'Taffy' Jones was sprinting towards the oncoming lumbering tank carrying a couple of grenades. Taking out the mighty monster would mean certain victory for our British lads. However, just as Sergeant Jones neared the tank, it began to swivel its gun turret towards the oncoming Tommy. We gasped. Surely the end was nigh!

Suddenly, salvation was at hand. With two ominous thuds, followed by a tearing noise, the Panza tank lost part of its turret. We had won! The cinema erupted. Actually, Philip Lynn had won. Overcome with excitement, and sitting in the centre front row of the stalls, he had hurled his interval snack – a large Jaffa orange and a small bottle of dandelion and burdock – straight at the menacing tank and, more to the point, at the cinema screen! The tearing noise, we later realised, had been the screen ripping.

The loud cheers from the audience were short-lived when the house lights suddenly came on, the film stopped, and a fuming cinema manager sprinted down the aisle towards the front of the stalls. There was an audible gasp as we realised that a large, jagged hole had now appeared in the centre of the wide screen and the Nazi army was nowhere to be seen. Philip, meanwhile, had wriggled his way under the seats to the rear of the stalls to escape, and sat back watching the action as the fuming cinema manager began an interrogation to find out the identity of the front row 'bomb thrower'! He never did.

The manager then cancelled the morning matinee, as well as the rest of the weekend's performances. He also had to order a replacement film screen, which luckily was installed just in time for the following Monday evening's movie.

Although we had been robbed of the final ten minutes or so of the film, it really did not matter, for wasn't the battle finally won, with the dangerous Panza tank put out of action? Undoubtedly, Philip Lynn was a hero! Not only had he stopped the Nazi army single-handedly, he had also escaped undetected from the scene of his triumph. For many weeks afterwards we called him Sergeant Lynn, which he proudly played up to. He even persuaded his mam, who did not realise the significance of his new nickname, to sew three chevrons onto his shirtsleeve!

Our Plaza adventures were soon to stop, however, when disaster struck one Thursday evening. A fire engine, siren whailing raced towards the centre of town, racing towards the Plaza cinema which was on fire and burning out of control. The next morning we gathered beside the burnt-out remains, shocked at the state of the once-proud cinema. Suddenly the two remaining theatres became the focus of the town's attention and huge queues formed outside of both cinemas that evening, particularly at the Empire cinema where a repeat of *Stagecoach*, starring John Wayne, was the main feature film showing.

Well before the film was due to start, the queue outside the Empire stretched some distance from the cinema doors, past Cuby's the chemist and even reaching as far as the town square Wesley Place, many yards up Church Street! Suddenly, Bob Armstrong, the manager of the Empire cinema, appeared and began to stride up the length of the queue. Mr Armstrong was what my mam called an 'eccentric character'. In order to drum up customers, he often stood outside the front entrance of his cinema dressed up in a costume linked to the theme of that week's feature film. Sometimes he would disguise himself as a pirate with a patch over his left eye and a stuffed parrot clinging to his shoulder or, as on this occasion, as John Wayne in a black, leather-tasseled jacket and trousers, high-heeled boots with shining spurs, a large Stetson set at a jaunty angle and a fancy gun belt (complete with two holstered 'cap-charged' Colt revolvers).

Ignoring the applause from the front section of the huge queue, he marched up Church Street with a typical John Wayne rolling swagger. Halting halfway up the massive line and firing both toy pistols into the air, he immediately gained the attention of the jostling crowd and all passers-by. 'Reet!' he shouted. 'Aal ye Plaza lot, aah want ye te move te the back of the queue. Yee may not 'ave a picture hoose, but this doesn't give ye the right to squeeze oot me regulars!' and with that he began to call out the names of some of his loyal Empire customers. 'Bella Smith an' Geordie Waggot – aah see yer reet at the back! Cum on doon!' he exclaimed as he slowly extracted his regular Empire film customers one by one, much to the dismay of the remaining 'Plaza lot', who found themselves being shuffled back towards the end of the queue.

As good as his word, Mr Armstrong continued to favour his loyal followers over the next few weeks. However, the queues to the Empire started to shrink when most of the Plaza-less townsfolk, despite their dislike of Mr Smolt, began to go to the Pavilion more often, which, after all, was a more comfortable and clean cinema than the Empire and it also had more interesting programmes of films.

It was not until a few months later that the Plaza cinema re-opened with a grand gala night, attended by most of the town's important people, including the leader of the town council, the chief of the fire service (perhaps he was just checking the safety of the cinema?) and many of the town's tradesmen. One hour before the opening ceremony, a local colliery band entertained the milling crowds outside – including my Mary Street pals and me – and the cinema entrance was covered in ribbons and multi-coloured balloons (which we all agreed looked terrific). After much speechmaking the ceremony ended and the packed theatre eventually settled down to the smell of fresh paint, to enjoy the first feature film of the newly-built Plaza cinema, aptly called *The Flames Below*!

Chapter Eight

Celebrations

Victory! We had won! The war in Europe was over! A wave of joy swept the town as church bells rang out in celebration. Everyone seemed to have smiles on their faces and a jaunt to their step. Even Aunty 'Nipped-In Bette' was seen to have a wide, toothy grin through her normally tightly pursed lips (perhaps she could, after all, eat normally without the aid of a straw?).

The main public celebrations were to be in two or three open-air street parties in the lower part of town, although for some reason the people of Mary Street and many of its sloping, neighbouring streets were not to follow suit. Despite my questioning – 'If they can hold a party, why can't we?' – Mam's only answer was that as our street was on such a steep bank, we would not be able to place anything on the tables outside without everything tumbling off. My suggestion that I could put all my party food in an empty shoebox to make up for sitting at an angle was dismissed! My sister later told me that it was more likely that as we were still struggling to put food on the table at home for ourselves, we would have a hard time coming up with enough food for a party. Despite the war being over, severe rationing was still in place.

Gathering for a pow-wow summit later that day, my pals and I decided that we would still celebrate – at a street party no less – even if there was not going to be a party on Mary Street itself. Although many of our pals, families and neighbours had been invited to less exciting celebrations, we decided we wanted our own Mary Street party.

So, the day that the street party celebrations dawned, we brave Apaches met at the bottom of the Dene. We had agreed that we would sneak into the other street parties in pairs, targeting all three street parties at the same time. However, like our brave and clever Apache brothers, we would hold off striking until the parties were in full swing, judging that everyone would be far too busy with their sandwiches and whatever cakes had been made, as well as the grown-ups being too merry with their 'white man's firewater' to notice us. (Earlier that morning, on a planned scouting mission, Crazy Hands had seen during his early morning paper-round several barrels of beer and cider being trundled towards where the street parties were taking place, so we were confident in our plans.)

The sign for the celebrations to start was the town's air-raid siren going off at precisely 1.00 p.m. Soon the frenzied feasting and drinking was in full swing, with the raucous marching tune of *Onward Christian Soldiers* being belted out enthusiastically by the local Salvation Army band. Everyone was determined to enjoy themselves, except perhaps Jackie Waggot, the local town drunk, who had decided to start celebrating early and was found snoring at ten minutes past one underneath one of the trestle tables.

After about an hour had passed – and, we hoped, with the food still being eaten – our Apache hunting party split into three groups of two ready to start our raid. My companion was Running Brave and, because of his speed, I made him carry the bag into which we would stash our filched party food. Even if we were caught, we thought that not even an adult, sober or otherwise, would be able to lay a hand on Running Brave.

The raid went off without a hitch and to our delight was a terrific success. No-one questioned or even noticed our presence – the other children were too busy scoffing their heads off, the adults laughing loudly, drowning out the attempts of the Salvation Army band, who carried on playing despite all the screaming, shouting and singing. I was astonished at the range of food still piled high on the tables. My favourites – jam tarts, cream (real!) cakes and iced currant buns – sat among piles of sandwiches (some filled with salmon (tinned) or large slices of Spam and even corned beef!).

Standing next to a large-chested woman, I slowly recognised her as one of my fellow shoppers from the Co-op shops – there she had always worn a stained, black dress and hair-curlers under a black headscarf (which I had assumed were a permanent fashion fixture), but now she was transformed, wearing a light flowery dress, high-heeled shoes and she had beautiful red hair cascading down her back. Turning to one of her friends who was helping to keep the table tidy, she said, 'Aaal this luvely grub, Annie! Whey weeve waited oour six years fur this spread, saving our best rations just for this moment – an' aaal tell yee it was worth it!' And with that, she was whisked away by a fellow partygoer to dance in the middle of the street to *Jesus Wants Me for a Sunbeam*, even introducing a dancing rhythm to the sombre Salvation Army hymn!

As the party got noisier, the ghost-like Apache Braves raided the long trestle tables, stashing away the odd bits of food – a sandwich here, an iced bun there – of which there were still piles. Later on, Brave Buffalo told us he had been collared by one of the grown-ups with a 'Yee look as if yee got nee flesh on yur bones! Sit here, bonny lad, an' git stuck in an' help yoursell", which of course he did, not forgetting to put several items into his bag as well!

Having filled our bags, we made our way to our Summerhill reservation to count our loot. Emptying it all into a pile, we smiled gleefully. Apart from Brave Buffalo we had not eaten a morsel, so not being able to wait any longer we all fell onto the food ravenously, tucking into our ill-gotten gains and enjoying the best tea most of us had ever had.

Later on at home, each of our mams was surprised that we were not too hungry, and the next day they feared we had all been struck down by a bug, because none of us were well enough to do our choir duties during that Sunday's matins service. Our poor stomachs had rebelled at the sudden introduction of so much rich food and we were all left groaning in our beds.

Although we were all suffering for our crimes – Chief Brown Legs (Dickie Hudson) was ill for two days and even missed school on the following Monday – none of us felt a scrap of guilt. As Brave Buffalo said later when we all met up again, 'Wasn't the grub free and nee money needed?' adding wisely (we thought) that, 'It was not thur same as stealing from a shop!'

*   *   *

The biggest event of the year for me next to Christmas was Bonfire Night. However, because of the war and the blackout, my second favourite celebration had been stopped. Now, though, the war was over and we could have Bonfire Night again!

My pals and I started to gather material for our Guy Fawkes beacon several weeks before the fifth of November and this needed careful military planning. Three days before the big night, we set up a guard system to protect all that we had gathered, which involved every member of the Mary Street gang. Our security began straight after school and our tea-time snack and lasted until 9.00 p.m. The reason for this was because of the Railway Street gang, who were like the rustlers we had seen countless times in our Plaza cinema matinees – stealing the old homesteader's few cattle and burning his barn.

The Railway Street Gang – or the 'Down-streeters' as we nicknamed them – were a menace and before the banning of Bonfire Night had attacked and removed large sections of competitive bonfires throughout the area, including our very own. They would raid rival bonfires under the cover of darkness and melt away with their spoils into the night. Not surprisingly, the Railway Street bonfire was always the biggest one in town, yet because of their rustling tactics the gang only needed to build it a couple of days before the fifth of November.

However, despite our best efforts to keep our bonfire guarded, our security plan had a problem – our parents' insistence that we went to bed no later than 8.00 p.m. This meant that the bonfire was exposed and vulnerable to any attack after this hour. Luckily Philip Lynn came up with an answer. Although, like all of us, he was sent to bed around 8.00 p.m., for the three nights before the event, Philip went to bed fully clothed, threatening his four younger siblings (who shared his bed) with death if they told on him. Then, each evening he would slip out of the bedroom, through the half-open sash window at the top of the stairs and down the drain pipe, before sprinting to the piece of wasteland at the top of Mary Street where we had built our bonfire. There he would settle down at the base of the bonfire chewing an apple or some other loot he had filched earlier from the kitchen.

Brave Buffalo later claimed that he had guarded the bonfire right up to St Cuthbert's midnight church chimes, and, apart from one dangerous moment when he had accidentally stood on a cat in his backyard (causing his dad to open the window of his bedroom and sling a boot at him) he was able to sneak back undetected into the house each night.

So, in the event of a Railway Street gang attack, we felt we were prepared. We had already placed a small pile of soot near the edge of the bonfire with which the guards could blacken their faces and so camouflage their presence – a tip we had picked up after seeing a recent movie at the Empire cinema where 'face-blackened' British commandos had heroically attacked a German gun position, We had also agreed that in the event of an attack, the sentry would be armed with a number of lethal 'Jumpy Jacks' – a small concertina-shaped cartridge, about two inches in length, which despite its small size created several loud cracking explosions, and was our favourite firework. Finally it was agreed that all soldiers would carry an alarm device – a tin whistle on a piece of string around the neck. We were ready!

Because Bonfire Night happened to be on a Saturday, we started guarding our bonfire from the Thursday before in the hopes of fending off an attack. My house was only a hundred yards or so from the bonfire site and, tossing and turning, I found it difficult to get to sleep. Would they attack? Would our fellow Apache, Brave Buffalo, successfully defend the beacon? Eventually I fell asleep and dreamt of riding with Geronimo and his brave warriors through the Railway Street camp, spread-eagling all their gang and destroying their large bonfire!

The next morning before school I rushed to the top of Mary Street and was delighted to see the bonfire intact. Later, during school playtime, Brave Buffalo explained that he had thought he had heard rustlers creeping towards him, so he had given a blast on his whistle and they had scampered! The following two evenings, according to Philip, resulted in further attempts to plunder our bonfire but he bravely fought them off with two Jumpy Jacks and a volley of whistling. We were all relieved. The bonfire was safe, and once again Brave Buffalo was a hero!

To make sure our bonfire was the best ever, we had all been collecting every item of burnable material we could get our hands on in the few weeks leading up to Bonfire Night. As a result, our bonfire grew from a small three-foot pile to a neck-craning tower over twenty feet high. We had come up with various methods for collecting fuel, from calling at every house in the area to searching the local woods and hedgerows, and Billie Hutchinson had even discovered the huge prize of a large mattress on the town rubbish tips, which he proudly presented to the rest of us. Billie was also lucky to be able to commandeer the services of Isaac Holmes the coalman to transport his prize. Being a friend of Billie's dad, Issac readily agreed to allow us the use of his trusty horse and cart.

I would say, however, that the best addition to our bonfire was a large rocking chair, which became the focus of the entire project, for here would sit the dummy of Mr Guy Fawkes himself (or Hitler, as we had decided). This treasure was presented to the gang by Dickie Biggins. Dickie often used to run errands for the ancient Mrs Maughan (who lived six doors up from me on Mary Street) and when he asked her if she would consider contributing any unwanted items for the bonfire, she offered him the rocking chair, which was stored in her backyard shed. The chair had not been used for several years and Mrs Maughan told Dickie that it was downright too dangerous for both herself and her husband Seth (who was just as ancient). Apparently the last time he had sat in it, it had been at least half an hour before he could struggle to his feet again, feeling quite seasick!

The most important part of the bonfire, however, was of course the Guy (Hitler). Ours had to be perfect, and it was given to us by Mrs Embleton (whose eldest son, Bob, was in charge of the Co-op grocery wagon). Mrs Embleton lived in the bottom house in Polmaise Street, right next to the bonfire site, and every year she had kindly supplied the gang with the traditional Guy for our bonfire. Bob told us that his mam used old tea cosies, odd socks, torn sheets and straw to make the Guy, and this year she had also stuffed inside a pair of Bob's about-to-be discarded overalls, which had seen better days.

The head of our tyrant Hitler was to be a large turnip with gouged-out eyes filled with two glass alleys (marbles – the best for the job) and with a sooty moustache painted on. Fixed firmly on top would be a large, handle-less white po (chamber pot), which we thought looked like a German soldier's helmet.

We were extremely proud of our bonfire, which was all the more eye-catching with our Herr Hitler sitting defiantly on his throne – the rocking chair. This sat on top of our collection of junk, which included strips of 'Tary-Toot' (roof covering) and a jumble of household items, from some old, warped 'posh-sticks' – wooden staffs used for beating laundry – to several snapped clothes props, which would no longer support the Monday morning street washing-lines.

We were all feverishly counting down to Saturday, and finally the great day arrived. My pals and I had all cajoled and pleaded to our parents over the preceding week for extra pocket money to buy a variety of fireworks – these were important for the celebrations to highlight all our efforts once the ceremonial lighting of the massive bonfire had been done. This was to take place at 6.00 p.m. and the honour of lighting the bonfire was traditionally given to the oldest residents of the street, which this year were Mr and Mrs Maughan, donors of the magnificent rocking chair. However, Mr and Mrs Maughan were not quite up to walking up the steep incline of the street to do the honours, after all they were both at least 150 years old, and Dickie Hudson said that perhaps they were even older. For he had recently seen a film featuring, Wise Owl', grandmother of the great Apache Chief Geronimo, whose wizzened features reminded him of Mrs Maughan. Dickie said Wise Owl had declared, when addressing the tribe council, that she was even older than the stars!

So, with Mr and Mrs Maughan out of the picture, the honour of lighting the Mary Street bonfire went to the next elderly street resident, old Mr Burns, who claimed to be over one hundred years old – a whole lot younger than 150 years we all agreed – and who was considered quite sprightly for his age by my mam, seeing as he was to walk without the aid of a walking stick. Mr Burns was a kindly soul, who continually sucked at his clay pipe – this only emitted smoke on the rare occasions he was given a gift of tobacco on his birthday and at Christmas time from the Salvation Army. Mr Burns happily accepted the honour of the lighting up ceremony and on Saturday evening was the first of the locals to appear at our bonfire, dressed in his Sunday suit and chewing on the end of his smokeless clay pipe.

The fireworks portion of our evening was to consist of all the fireworks that our pocket money could buy. Following our individual firework expeditions to Jack Brunton's, the town's comic and newspaper shop in Church Street, we had all agreed to meet in Billie Hutchinson's backyard to compare our choice of ammunition. I presented two rockets, two bags of sparklers, a volcano and four silver fountains. Billie had invested in one rocket (slightly bigger than mine), three Catherine wheels and three whiz-bangs, while his younger brother Alan showed off a bag of sparklers and two packets of London Lights. The rest of the gang started to produce similar fireworks, and then it was Philip Lynn's turn. He proceeded to open a large paper bag containing to our astonishment dozens of lethal Jumpy Jacks, which must have cost him a fortune! He averted our gasps by saying, with an innocent smile, that he had found them in the back street at the rear of Jack Brunton's shop!

Rumour afterwards linked his good fortune to his elder sister Peggy, who happened to work part-time in the paper shop. Apparently, one day on emptying the shop rubbish into the bins at the rear, she had inadvertently thrown out the bag of Jumpy Jacks whilst Philip mysteriously happened to be meandering past at the same time! It was not the only mistake that Peggy was to make, and she was soon swapping jobs (fired) and was thereafter seen working as a bottle washer in Howie's Dairy opposite the railway station.

So, bolstered by the thought of the huge hoard of fireworks we had collected, I wandered up to the bonfire after 5.00 p.m. on Saturday evening, with my fireworks and two potatoes (which I hoped to roast in the dying embers of the fire later on). On reaching the top of Mary street and turning left towards the bonfire, I could see by the glow of the streetlight at the bottom of Polmaise Street that all was not well. As I neared the bonfire, rubbing my eyes to make sure, I saw that the wonderful rocking chair had disappeared, leaving Herr Hitler squatting unsteadily on the summit, wedged between two large pieces of timber. I was horrified. Surely the Railway Street Gang had not paid a night-time visit? If they had, surely they would have been spotted by our brave sentry? And in any case, surely they would have carted away more than a single chair for their own needs!

Just then the rest of the gang arrived and, like me, they were shocked and upset. Brave Buffalo confirmed that on finishing his sentry duties the previous night the throne had still been there. No one could supply an answer to the mystery of the disappearing rocking chair, and, as it happens, we weren't to solve the puzzle until several weeks later.

In the meantime, with a Dunkirk-like spirit, we started the evening's entertainment and, with loud applause from the gathering crowd, Mr Burns thrust the ignited torch (a clothes prop with a paraffin-soaked rag tied to the end) into the base of the bonfire. With a whoosh, the flames soon climbed up to the top of the pyre and enveloped the throne-less Hitler. After everyone admired our many weeks worth of effort burning merrily away, we eagerly started the fireworks part of the evening. Even the sight of Herr Hitler tumbling down within seconds of the fire starting was soon out of our minds as the variety of fireworks caused great joy and satisfaction to the large crowd of neighbours and their smaller children, who often shrieked in terror when a rocket went off into one of the trees growing close to the bonfire site.

Soon after this, Brave Buffalo caused huge mayhem with his arsenal of Jumpy Jacks by popping a couple through the letterbox of the nearby house of Darkie Dallas, as well as slipping several into the coat pockets of the attending mams with their small children. He also threw several directly into the bonfire itself, causing glowing debris to fly out quite dangerously.

The evening ended as the bonfire slowly shrank into hot glowing embers with Herr Hitler's helmet having bounced down clear of the inferno to lie smoldering near the fence at the edge of the wasteland. One by one everyone sauntered home with smoke in their hair, faces slightly reddened by the heat from the bonfire and in my case a sore mouth through eating a charred potato too hot for consumption. The only member of the gang who did not stay for the end of the festivities had departed early on in the evening – having fled the anger of a couple of angry mams with their coat pockets still smoldering! Brave Buffalo had struck again!

A few weeks after Bonfire Night, I called at Philip Lynn's house to see if he was in, but there was no response to my shouted: 'Philip, Philip, are you coming out to play?', only silence. Then, after more calling, Mrs Lynn shouted down from the upstairs bedroom: 'He's next doo-or at his granma's hoose!' I had never entered this tiny, two-down/two-up terraced house before, so I stood outside it shouting for Philip, waiting for a reply to my calls to come out and play. However when this failed to work I decided, after some hesitation, to enter through the scullery's open door, calling out

'Hello?' as I went in. Only silence met my entry into the scullery, so I continued on into the living room.

This too, however, was empty and I could smell that the whole place reeked of a sickly, stale sweat, dog's poo and rotting cabbage. There were no pictures on the walls, which were covered with a dull-patterned wallpaper and, around the doors, the wallpaper was smeared with oily finger marks, whilst elsewhere on the walls huge patches of it had been peeled off revealing the original plaster beneath. Hanging from the ceiling was a solitary gas mantle, which when lit, I assumed would highlight the holed, torn, grey mesh curtains and the filthy, uneven, linoleum floor. A large wooden table sat in the centre of the room and I could see that its once highly carved and decorated legs were now covered in scratches – evidence of an attack by a sabre-toothed tiger, I imagined with a shiver.

Surrounding the table were three matching upright padded chairs, which had seen better days as their lining was clearly peeping out. A single, wooden cracket stool, showing similar scars to the table legs, stood in front of the glowing, open coal fire, and a large blackened kettle puffed wisps of steam to the left of a black lead range. I could also see on the mantelpiece a grinning Toby jug, several clay pipes and a large wooden-cased clock without its glass face. However, what really caught my eye was a large piece of furniture standing proudly in the far corner of the room: our bonfire's rocking chair! With astonishment, I shook my head. Brave Buffalo had struck again!

Chapter Nine

The Apache Trail

Black Hawk – John Solomon
Brave Buffalo – Philip Lynn
Crazy Hands – Billie Hutchinson
Running Brave – Alan Dodds
Chief Brown Legs – Dickie Hudson
Big Wigwam Callaghan – Fatty Callaghan (guest
 Apache)

I was standing next to Fatty Callaghan in the queue at Worley's the baker's when he asked me if I thought the Mary Street gang would be interested in using a large tent over the weekend. Fatty said that the tent was being looked after by his older brother, a member of the local Scouts, who had their HQ in a house next to Blaydon's New Inn. The Scouts' tent had needed a good airing after being soaked at a rain-drenched camp at Ryton Willows the previous weekend, and it was now available to be used. I responded to the idea with enthusiasm and agreed to look after the tent over the weekend, promising to return it to his backyard on Sunday night.

Eager to tell the rest of the gang of our good fortune, I quickly finished my shopping chores and raced home, where I contacted all of the Mary Street gang. We agreed to hold a pow-wow the following afternoon at Summerhill, at 5.00 p.m. sharp. Apart from the recently forgiven Dickie Biggins (who had caused our blood brothers ceremony to fall apart, and who now had the lame excuse that he had to look after his ill pet dog) we all agreed that an Apache camp with the use of a large wigwam, in or around Stella Woods this coming Saturday evening, would be thrilling. This was despite the fact that Crazy Hands had spotted the Railway Street gang camping near Stoney's pond only a few hundred yards from the outer fringes of the woods the previous weekend.

The next day at our pow-wow, we each confirmed that our parents had agreed to the expedition taking place. Now, as the dangers of the wartime bombing were over, we were each being encouraged to cut the apron strings, and we were eagerly looking forward to our first time ever away from home. It was as if we were finally taking our first steps towards manhood!

That evening I called at Fatty Callaghan's house to see the tent. Even the fact that I had to agree to his older brother's condition that Fatty would have to join the expedition did not dim my delight at the upcoming adventure. Fatty Callaghan was around the same age as the rest of us, but he had always been on the fringe of the Mary Street activities because his family was Roman Catholic. Even so, he seemed quite a pleasant lad to me, especially as he often agreed to share his gobstoppers, so I had no problem with Fatty joining in with our adventure. He had been the means of giving the Mary Street gang a wigwam, so I thought Catholics couldn't be so bad after all!

I impatiently waited for Saturday afternoon to arrive, when we would all gather outside Fatty Callaghan's backyard. Finally, the school week was over and the gang took delivery of the (still) slightly damp tent from Fatty's older brother, with the help of my dad's two-wheeled pigeon-basket cart to carry it. Our adventure could begin! Along with my fellow braves, I placed on top of the cart my makeshift sleeping bag with a cardboard box containing my essential picnic-type rations hidden inside. Setting out in good heart with my pals, we headed towards Stella Woods. I joined in with my fellow warriors, joshing and chortling at the headgear of Running Brave – Alan Dodds – who was wearing a pith helmet (discovered and filched from the basement of the Church Hall from among the props kept for church pageants). Despite our increasingly hilarious ridicule, Alan insisted on wearing the helmet, even though we pointed out that we were brave Indians on our way to an Apache reservation and not on a safari in the jungle!

It was a delightful sunny and warm autumn afternoon as we started our adventure and, taking turns in pairs, we pushed the loaded cart at great speed down the bank, narrowly missing Mrs Hymers as she turned the corner at the bottom of Mary Street. Running along with the cart, we left Mrs Hymers behind leaning against the church wall and waving angrily after us with her walking stick. Our brave Apache band sped through town with the loaded cart, running mostly in single file, whooping like the true warriors we were, although only Brave Buffalo sported dabs of sooty black war paint on his forehead and cheeks. The rear of our war-party was brought up by the 'Pith Helmet' – as we had taken to calling Running Brave – who occasionally tripped over a kerb as the large helmet slipped over his eyes, causing us to snort with laughter.

Our speed slowed when we got to the steep slope leading up to Summerhill – it took the efforts of nearly the entire tribe to keep the cart going forward. The only member of our war-party not helping in our hard-pressed efforts to reach the top of the bank was Fatty Callaghan, who had decided to pull rank on us as the keeper of the wigwam and had excused himself from cart duty. Instead he chose to walk ahead of us, waving a white handkerchief on the pretext that he was acting as a traffic safety guide. The rest of the tribe was not impressed. Grunting up the hill, we muttered darkly between deep breaths, but without his brother's tent the camp would never have taken place, so we therefore grudgingly agreed not to challenge him. However, this did not satisfy Brave Buffalo, who threatened to take Fatty's scalp at the first opportunity!

Our arrival at Stella Woods did much to cheer everyone up and we immediately started to search the thickly wooded area for a site to pitch our wigwam. However, apart from the overgrown path running through the centre of the woods we failed to locate a suitable flat area not obstructed by trees, nettle beds or thorny shrubs. Eventually we all agreed that we should abandon our woodland campsite and head back towards Summerhill to set up camp in the area below its summit in Howie's Field – a large stretch of buttercupped meadow overlooking the River Tyne. After much bickering over the best site, it was finally decided that we should pitch our tent in the lee of Summerhill in the corner of the meadow, just next to the allotments nestling in the shadow of the hill.

By this time we were overheating with the hot sun and all our sweaty efforts of pushing the cart, and we discarded our by-now soaked shirts. Pulling the cart over the bumpy field, we finally found an ideal spot for the camp on a level piece of land with short-cropped grass and a good view of the River Tyne, which Brave Buffalo pointed out was a good place from which to see any attacks by rival Indians coming along the river in silent, menacing canoes. We then set about erecting the tent, with Fatty Callaghan attempting to direct the operations. These were based on the instructions his brother had passed on to him the night before, but he often became confused and kept repeating, 'No, not that way up – this way up!' and 'No, that's upside down!'

After at least an hour of much pulling and pushing of damp canvas, the semblance of our home for the night began to take shape, although our efforts had not been helped by Chief Brown Legs – Dickie Hudson – who had mislaid one of the important tent poles in the long grass, having used the pole to practise for the next Olympic Games javelin event. At last, however, our wigwam was up! We all gave a great cheer and then ran round the tent howling out Apache-style yells.

From the outside, the tent looked like a misshapen survivor of a cattle stampede, with the canvas roof hanging down in folds. Still, despite its somewhat drunken appearance, the inside of the wigwam was quite large, and although for some reason we were only able to squeeze through a tiny narrow entrance one at a time to enter, we all stood inside to admire our efforts (ignoring the fact that our heads brushed the low canvas ceiling and the inner tent walls billowed alarmingly inwards as the outside breeze increased).

Grinning delightedly, we all praised Fatty Callaghan for his skill as a number one wigwam builder and promptly called him 'Big Wigwam Callaghan' or WC for short, which also reflected his ability to pee the longest in a recent contest we had had overlooking 'The Dats', a steep, wooded slope in Stella Woods. WC was delighted, finding his new nickname far more to his liking than 'Fatty'. It was also decided that as WC had opted out of the strenuous hill climb, he would be given the job of searching the meadow for some wild and delightfully sweet pignuts instead – something we all agreed would go down well with our evening meal.

The remainder of the afternoon was a joyous programme of fun and games, ending in the Summerhill Olympic Games, featuring all the accepted field events. It was universally agreed that the outright winner would be the contestant who won the most individual events. It was further agreed by all that ginger-haired Billie Hutchinson – named Crazy Hands because he had double-jointed fingers – would be the sole umpire of the games, as he had brought along his dad's pocket-watch (which even though it didn't have a glass face, still ticked well and had a second hand – ideal for the running contests).

Let the Games begin! The first event was the tree-climbing competition, with the winner being the one who could climb the nearby pine tree in the shortest time. Each competitor had to touch the rook's nest at the top of the tree before climbing down. I was confident in this event because the chosen tree had a ladder-like branch structure and looked easy to climb. However, despite my best efforts, the prize went to Brave Buffalo. The next two events – the short sprint and middle distance races – were also both won by Brave Buffalo as Running Brave had been injured earlier by the cart running over his foot. The javelin contest – using a pointed, straight elderberry branch as a javelin – was won not surprisingly by Chief Brown Legs. However, his victory was greeted by a chorus of boos from everyone else because, unlike his competitors, he had been practising the event most of the afternoon.

Then came the long jump event at the top of the meadow, and this was won by Brave Buffalo. Shot putt or 'throwing the rock' proved simple for WC, who won by several yards, and 'holding-the-breath-the-longest' was won by Running Brave. Finally, came the difficult field walk event – where the winner would be the one who could walk in the straightest line down the centre of the field, blindfolded! Black Hawk (myself) was the first to enter and, following only a few minutes, I found myself totally lost and without direction, veering off into a gorse bush with no warning apart from the howls of laughter from the audience. This fiendish event proved the undoing for many brave Apaches, but the eventual winner was ... Brave Buffalo (who else?!), who miraculously completed several hundred yards in a dead straight line before getting lost.

So, Brave Buffalo was crowned the overall Olympic winner, and we christened him the 'O*LYNN*PIC CHAMPION'! However, soon after, questions were asked about the tightness of his blindfold, and much bickering was only avoided by Crazy Hands shouting, 'Lets 'ave wore dinna!' This announcement was cheered and we all dived for our individual packed rations, having agreed earlier that as true Apaches we should share the food and drink amongst us. Sitting cross-legged outside the wigwam, we each opened our large, string-tied, brown paper bags and cardboard boxes – carefully packed by our parents with a mouthwatering mix of food (sandwiches), which at first glance seemed enough to last for a whole week, never mind a short weekend!

When all the provisions were placed on the short grass in front of us, we counted to ten and then all dived in without ceremony to sate our starving appetites. Our two-course field menu looked like this:

Selection Of Sandwiches

(thickness varies, but mostly doorstoppers)

Sliced Tomato and Spam – (Mrs Dodds)

Fish Paste – (Mrs Hutchinson)

Blackberry Jam – (Mrs Hudson)

Condensed Milk – (Mrs Callaghan)

Margarine and Sugar – (Mrs Lynn)

Cold Rice Pudding (Mrs Callaghan again, perhaps reflecting her son's capacity!)

Potted Meat – (Mrs Solomon)

Dessert

A mixture of apples and pears, and freshly dug, local pignuts (four each)

We soon quenched our thirst with a variety of pop – lemonade, dandelion and burdock, Tizer, cream soda and home-made ginger beer, the latter being in a large, stone-coloured earthenware jug with a cork stopper, kindly given to me by our next-door neighbour Mr 'Storyteller' Richardson, with the request that I return the jug. The ginger beer proved to be the most popular of the drinks and we passed the jug around copying the Apache style of drinking 'firewater' by pouring the liquid straight into our mouths with the jug held several inches above our faces. Running Brave only succeeded in showering his head, and for his wastefullnes was only allowed to drink from the Tizer bottle.

After the second round of drinking, Crazy Hands declared with a giggle that he was feeling drunk, even though the ginger beer had no alcohol in it. However, his 'happy' state was infectious and soon we all believed we were under the influence too, becoming boisterous and laughing non-stop. Brave Buffalo then decided that it was the right time to perform the traditional war dance and we all leapt to our feet with enthusiasm and formed a (drunken) circle. Banging sticks together, we began stamping our feet to a well-rehearsed rhythmic chant that we had copied from a matinée film we had seen at the Plaza cinema.

Then, exhausted, we all flopped down onto the now flattened circle of grass and wolfed down the remainder of our food, apart from a small supply of potatoes, which we were saving for our late supper before bedtime. Earlier, during our meal, we had told WC off for stuffing his face with food so that he could eat an unfair share of the banquet and, with the final item about to disappear down his throat, Brave Buffalo had snatched this last sandwich from him and given it to Running Brave, who chewed everything very slowly – apparently his mam having trained him to chew every morsel at least thirty times. During the war, most of us had learnt to eat our small rations very fast in the hope that someone would still have a leftover portion on their plate which we might then be given – but this never happened for Running Brave. Looking over at him, I thought that this was probably the reason why Running Brave was so fast – he hardly had any weight to carry when he ran!

Chief Brown Legs suddenly shouted, 'Let's 'ave a dip in the stream, lads!' and with this, we all set off whooping and hollering for the river, leaving Wigwam Callaghan to guard the camp. WC seemed quite happy to opt out, saying that he didn't much like water and was only forcibly introduced to it every Friday night at bath time.

Although I shared these feelings – disliking my own Friday night wash-night – the thought of a delicious dip in a clean, sparkling, running stream was certainly more attractive than my own Mary Street bath ritual. Here, I was forced to wash in a large tin bath, which usually hung on a nail in the backyard. This was carried inside the house, placed in front of a roaring coal fire in the living room and then filled with buckets of hot water from the gas boiler in our scullery. The old tin bath was filled in time for my dad's return home from his filthy and dusty labours at either the local brickworks, where he worked replacing the damaged interior walls of the huge brick kilns, or, during the war, at the arms factory. He therefore had the first go at the clear, piping hot water in the metal bath, followed straight after by my mam, then my sister and finally me – at which point I would sink into the still-warm, carbolic-scented water, but now with the surface covered with a thick layer of sludgy bubbles!

So, to me, the stream seemed to sparkle enticingly in the sunlight, and I leapt in along with my fellow warrior Braves, with much laughter and Apache yells. After our wild splashing, we clambered out and raced back to our camp, with the warm sun drying our glistening, naked bodies and with marauding midges chasing our every step. I arrived at the camp ahead of the gang and, slipping on my trousers and sandshoes, lay exhausted on the grass looking up at the clear blue sky. It seemed like the day would go on for ever and I sighed in contentment, warm in the friendship of my fellow Apaches.

When we had all arrived back at the camp and dressed, we decided to play a game of rounders using a large branch as the bat and the tennis ball Crazy Hands had found on the road outside the public tennis courts in Winlaton. Splitting into two teams, the game was ended finally when the ball was lost in the long grass, much to Crazy Hands' dismay. Then, as the sun began to set, we quickly built a log fire from the ready supply of surrounding kindling. This fire would not only supply the heat for roasting our late-night supper potatoes, but it would also protect our reservation from the night-time prowling timber wolves and bears.

We sat round the fire telling ghost stories – Brave Buffalo telling one that sent shivers through me – but these were quickly forgotten as we ate a delicious roast potato supper, where I burned my mouth. Then it was time to turn in, with most of us yawning, and according to Crazy Hands' watch it was past 10.00 p.m.!

We soon unfolded our bedding in the wigwam. I had brought a thick woollen blanket which my mam had sewn together with twine to form a sleeping bag. Brave Buffalo had packed his dad's buttoned-up Home Guard army overcoat, which he could only enter by way of the hem, as the rusty brass buttons were impossible to unfasten. Big Wigwam Callaghan boasted his brother's pucker Sea Scout sleeping bag, while both Running Brave and Chief Brown Legs produced similar large thick towels, not unlike my blanket, which were sewn tightly together on three sides to form neat sleeping bags.

When Crazy Hands untied the string holding his bedding together, several eyebrows were raised – for rolling out in front of him was a small, thin, ragged and stained eiderdown, and tucked inside that was a woman's pink negligee! 'Shit!' he cursed, which took us all by surprise, as swearing was very rare in our gang – the nearest to an oath we had ever got was when Brave Buffalo shouted 'Bum!' to the postman. Regaining his self-control, Crazy Hands snorted with laughter – although his mam had insisted that he pack a pair of pyjamas, his younger brother Alan must have swapped them for his mam's nightie when he was not looking. He vowed he would get his revenge on the little snot when he got back home. In the meantime he shrugged that it really made no difference, as surely Apaches were not pyjama-wearers anyway! We agreed with this heartily, as we had all decided, following a cowboys and Indians matinee film, to do without Western sleeping clothes and sleep naked. During this, however, I noticed that Big Wigwam Callaghan furtively pushed something down to the end of his sleeping bag, but not before I managed to glimpse the collar of a blue-and-white-striped pyjama jacket!

One by one we all settled down to various degrees of comfort – as the night drew in, the temperature seemed to drop and a chilly wind from the river began to seep through the narrow, flapping entrance of the wigwam (from where the canvas ties were missing). We had all bundled into the wigwam in any old way, and this had left Brave Buffalo next to the opening of the tent, exposed to the cold night breeze. However, within minutes of settling down and being irritated by the rustling of the tent flaps, Brave Buffalo had executed a Sahara Desert Roll (as seen in a recent war film), propelling himself over and over again, to much squawking and muffled shouts, until he had reached the far corner of the tent, still entombed in his thick, army greatcoat.

This sudden move forced everyone to shuffle forward reluctantly in the direction of the unwanted, chilly entrance, with the unfortunate Chief Brown Legs ending up right next to the opening. However, all was well, as he hardily expressed his satisfaction at his exposed sleeping position, adding that it would give him the chance of a fast escape from, say, an attack by the dreaded Railway Street gang, who were rumoured to enjoy camping nearby. As first out of the wigwam, Chief Brown Legs declared that he would also not be trapped by the resulting inferno from the fire of their burning arrows. There followed a deep collective intake of breath – perhaps he had made a wise move after all?

We all soon settled down again, however, apart from the aptly named WC, who occasionally rent the night's silence with his combination of high-pitched snoring and loud farts, we all slept soundly until dawn. Then, Chief Brown Legs suddenly sat up and, with a scream of 'Git oot lads, wear bin attacked!', promptly shot out of the tent. There followed a loud snort, a thunder of hoofs and a high-pitched whinnying: the Railway Street gang was attacking! Chief Brown Legs had been right!

We all tumbled from our bedding and, clawing over each other in real panic, poured out of the wigwam, shivering naked in the chilly morning air. Outside we were confronted by the sight of several large horses, but there was no sign of the menacing down-streeter Braves. Not waiting to find out, we all legged it in the direction of the fast-disappearing, bobbing white backside of Chief Brown Legs, who was rapidly making for the safety of Summerhill and the meadow boundary fence. Behind us, the animals were left to prod, sniff and trample all over the wigwam.

As we shivered together at the base of Summerhill, we heard shouting in the distance. As it got closer, we could see it was Mr Howie the milkman, owner of the meadow. 'Yee daft buggas!' he exclaimed. 'Yeel git yor death of cowld! Noo hadaway doon to yer tent and buuga oot of me field, 'cause yer scarin' me Gallowars!' He then strode towards his Gallowars (horses) and, with a flourish of his stick, corralled them back into the dairy yard, from where they had escaped. After that, he beckoned us to retrieve our belongings and so dismantle our camp.

In true Indian single file, and shivering, we approached our reservation. Dressing quickly, we had soon packed up all of our belongings and loaded them onto the cart. Apart from Chief Brown Leg's towelled sleeping bag, which was soiled with horse droppings, and Running Brave's badly dented pith helmet, our equipment seemed undamaged, but soon a distinct stench reached us from the sleeping bags – that of horse wee!

Gloomily, we trundled our way slowly through the empty streets of the town, a sorry sight; more like dishevelled tramps than brave fighting Apaches. The church clock struck 6.00 a.m. as we passed it, and soon we arrived at Mary Street – 'Heap big canny yame!' (home) as Crazy Hands exclaimed. Arriving at WC's house, we retrieved our bundles and off-loaded the wigwam. Then saying an Apache farewell, we departed and I wheeled the empty pigeon-cart ahead of me towards home.

Soon I was opening the backyard door and parking the cart in the shed next to the coalhouse, before dropping my smelly sleeping bag into the scullery. Although our dismal return to the street was in total contrast to our riotous departure, I was not too upset at the abrupt end of our adventure – it was reassuringly comforting to be home at number 27 again.

I crept upstairs silently, greeted by my dad's raucous snoring. Without disturbing my parents, I slipped noiselessly into my bed. Remembering our glorious adventures, I turned over with a contented sigh and, counting horses (who all seemed to have wild eyes and flared nostrils whilst jumping over a fence), soon drifted off into sleep.

Chapter Ten

The Un-co-operative Society?

The main shops of the Blaydon Co-operative Society were on Church Street, which linking with Wesley Square formed the main centre of the town's popular shopping area. Dad had told me that it was the second set of Co-operative shops to have been formed in the country, and that they had since become some of the busiest and most popular stores in Blaydon. However, Mam liked to shop there because not only was she able to buy well-priced goods in the form of the Co-op's own products, she, like the other shoppers who went there, was also regularly given a small sum of cash in the form of a 'divi' (or dividend).

This was based on a scheme the Co-op ran, where each member received a (small) sum of cash based on the amount of shopping they had bought over a quarter period at the store. This scheme had a famous saying that went with it – 'The more you buy, the more you save!' – that impressed upon all of us the need to keep the special receipts we received whenever we did any shopping at the Co-op. Such receipts were linked to a customer's own personal 'divi' number, which we had to tell the Co-op staff each time we bought something. Our membership number was 20153; my gran's was 20126 – it was essential that these were remembered and woe betide anyone if they forgot their personal membership number! So, not surprisingly, I had ours memorized off by heart and I could easily reel them off when needed.

From time to time, members had to submit their 'divi' chits to the Co-op's small bank premises and it was one of my chores to take our family's saved receipts to the 'divi' office. This was a small place on the corner of the Co-op building, just next to the Society's shoe shop. Seen from the outside, it looked dowdy and miserable and, I thought, quite sinister. There were no signs outside, and for some reason all the windows were camouflaged with a bilious-coloured green paint, blocking out the sunlight.

The inside of the office was miserable and poorly lit, with only the constant opening and closing of the entrance door allowing any sunlight to come in from the outside. Two spotty-faced clerks, who worked feverishly behind the single, tall counter, were seated on high-back chairs which were placed as close to the front door as possible, something which I imagined was just so they could get some light.

Of all the shopping errands I had to do, I disliked the Co-op 'divi run' (as I called it) the most. I often found myself queuing for up to half an hour at a time, and sometimes longer. The queues felt like they were never-ending and I always seemed to end up standing next to a large, fat woman dressed in mourning black, with curlers in her red hair and a hairy mole on her cheek, reeking of body odour and last night's stout.

To distract myself from the loathing I felt about this temporary captivity and its 'inmates', I often transported myself from the 'divi' office by imagining I was actually in a tough American state prison, as portrayed in a Hollywood film, which I had recently seen at the Plaza cinema. This film depicted San Quentin prison scenes of shuffling, menacing prisoners, with names like 'Scarface', who, manacled, could often be seen in a queue lining up for their meagre daily meal of cabbage and watery gravy.

On one particular morning, I was standing in this prison line, thinking up possible escape plans – hit the guards on the head and make a run for the door! – when I noticed that the fellow prisoner just ahead of me was not the usual 'hairy mole and curlers', but was, rather, a tall, unshaven, middle-aged man dressed in what I always thought of as the 'dole queue' uniform. Often, when passing the dole office opposite Blaydon Police Station, I could see that the majority of the 'out-of-workers' seemed to wear this very similar clothing. Most days, these men could be seen standing or leaning rather forlornly on the dole office's building wall, or on their 'hunkers' (squatting), waiting for the doors to open and they were frequently shrouded in a cloud of cigarette or pipe tobacco smoke as they waited.

This constant queue of 'malingerers', as my granddad called them, had a 'uniform' of soiled and bruised caps; white scarves that were tucked into the necks of their collarless shirts; gravy-stained waistcoats; baggy, dark trousers and scruffy black boots. In my Hollywood daydream, I therefore imagined the unshaven 'Dole Man' ahead of me as the menacing and vicious 'Scarface', so I kept as much distance between us in the queue as possible, thinking that if I accidentally touched him, he would attack me with the crude revolver he had secretly made in the San Quentin prison workshops. The spotty clerk behind the counter, shrouded in cigarette smoke, was the 'trusty' who served the food at the prison (and who had been planted on the inside to obtain Scarface's confession for an unresolved gang murder in San Francisco).

I often became so engrossed in my fantasy that I would soon lose all sense of time and surroundings, and this was just what I wanted because then it did not seem too long before I would find myself at the head of the queue. Indeed, I was often snapped out of my Walter Mitty fantasies by the aggressive, spotty 'trusty' snapping: 'Hurry up, lad! Stop daydreaming, we haven't aaal day, man!'

*   *   *

I was just about to turn twelve years old and, apart from bird's-nesting, one of my main interests was now professional football, something that I had recently been introduced to at a game at St James' Park (the home football ground of the famous team Newcastle United). This game had fired my imagination with possible future football glories and now my immediate ambition was to obtain the necessary soccer kit so I could achieve this.

One late Saturday afternoon, Dad arrived home with a huge smile on his face, carrying a large bunch of chrysanthemums. He had bought these prize flowers from his next-door allotment neighbour, Matty Johnson, (so he claimed!) and he thrust them into Mam's arms together with a five-pound note – a rarity in the Solomon household – before playfully slapping my mam's behind. Such a familiar display was unheard of, and indeed this was the first outward sign of affection I had seen between my parents! My dad always hid his feelings, whether it was within the four walls of our house or outside of them, and although I knew he was seen as a straightforward, plain-speaking chap who called a spade a spade, he was also somewhat reserved.

Dad quickly explained that he had just had two strokes of good fortune: his top racing-pigeon had won that day's prestigious Northern Counties Amalgamation championship race from France, and the racehorse he had backed that day had won 20–1. I was over the moon when he included me in his largesse by handing my sister and me seven shillings and sixpence each. This was the exact amount of money that I had been pestering him for over the last few weeks so that I could buy my first pair of football boots – and not just any old football boots, oh no, but the much-coveted brand: The Stanley Matthews 'International' football boot!

At last I could discard my old play boots and their holed soles containing temporary cardboard strips, and I could also stop wearing the sandshoes I often quickly wore out in just a couple of months. (Indeed, all my shoes suffered early wear and tear as a result of frequent attempts to propel a heavy cannonball-like object – a leather football – up our street; an object that only increased in weight in the wet weather. Such was the toughness of this ball, that when Dickie Hudson had once dared to head the sodden leather object on a wet afternoon, he had ended up at Doctor Morrison's surgery with a concussion. He never headed a football again, even on hot sunny dry days!)

So, the following Monday morning, being on holiday, I headed off for Church Street and the Co-op Society shoe shop immediately after breakfast, clutching my seven shillings and sixpence tightly in my hand. Here I had gazed lovingly at the centre of their shop window display: a pair of Stanley Matthews football boots. Over breakfast (my favourite of a slice of bread thickly spread with condensed milk), Mam had agreed with me that, as I was now growing up so fast, I should be able to go and buy my own shoes by myself for the first time ever. (Indeed, I was no longer the baby of the family because I now had a younger baby brother called Gordon. I remember many months before being invited upstairs to my mam's bedroom and being introduced to my new brother nestling next to my mam's bosom. I was astonished – not only had I been totally ignorant of this event, no one over the past year had talked about his impending arrival! To me he immediately seemed unfriendly, puffing out his red cheeks and thrusting out his tiny clenched hand. Little did I realize that this was a sign of his future musical talents playing the trombone!)[1]

So, here I was at the Co-op shoe shop and I entered completely alone. I found myself facing a large, glass-fronted counter at the rear of the shop. The shop walls were lined with row upon row of wooden shelving, stacked high with dozens of white shoe boxes all appearing to be of uniform size. With no one else in the shop, I guessed that I must be the first customer of the day and sat down on a bamboo chair next to a footrest with a string-attached shoehorn. Then I waited with trembling excitement for an assistant to appear.

Mam had advised me to buy the sports shoes of my choice, but in one size too big, saying that I would soon grow into them and that I could always fill in the space not occupied by my foot by wearing two or three pairs of football stockings! Unspoken in this, moreover, was the added bonus that this would save money in the long run. Mam was famous in our household for being very practical when it came to money and looking after the pennies in her tiny, weekly, household budget. When buying clothes, she often said, 'Ye must allways gan for the bigger sizes, cause ye'll soon graw into them in a few months' time.

---

[1] Gordon now in his sixties. became one of the great jazz exponents of this instrument and together with his band 'The River City Jazzmen', is still wowing audiences at his Tyneside gigs.

Anyway, this was obviously on her mind when a week earlier I had reluctantly gone with her to buy my first pair of long, 'grown-up' trousers at the town's drapery store, Armstrong & Bateman (Fashion Outfitters!). Here, the two glass front windows showed balaclavas perched on male dummy heads (which I thought were creepy because they lacked any eyes). These blind models also displayed thick, brown, corduroy trousers and matching brown boots. In the corner of the window was a female dummy who was draped in thick wool socks arranged like scarves around her bare shoulders. The dummy had lost her nose and I imagined that this must have happened in some scrap with a rival. Indeed, a likely rival stood just inside the shop's entrance where there was a tall, somewhat animated, male dummy, with evil flashing purple eyes, dressed in a thick, blue-and-white-striped set of pyjamas (and who, I thought, appeared to be none the worse for wear from this recent encounter, apart from a crack on his chin).

That day I needed a great deal of persuasion to go with my mam, as I argued that I was more than happy with my existing 'short pants'. I pointed out that long, 'clingy', ankle-length trousers would get in the way of my day-to-day running, climbing and jumping and I also felt that even though I was now nearly twelve years old, I was not at all ready to move up to long, grown-up trousers.

Despite all my arguments, however, we eventually left the store with a parcel containing a pair of long brown corduroy trousers and my first ever pair of braces. The next Sunday morning, I was told to wear the dreaded 'longs' for church matins service. On the way down the lane to St Cuthbert's Church, I found it very difficult to walk comfortably. The fly buttons seemed to be located in the higher regions of my chest – so much so that as a result there was no need to let out the braces beyond an inch to support the trousers. I also quickly discovered that trying to visit a gents' wall-mounted toilet was a no-go area, my private parts being suspended in one or other of the trouser legs and my underwear continually chasing around after them! 'Never mind!' Mam would exclaim, 'ye'll grow into them!' and so I would, I imagined, when many years had passed!

So now, alone in the Co-op shoe shop, and having sat on the hard, bamboo chair for several minutes without seeing anyone, I coughed loudly in the hopes of gaining some attention from a member of staff, who, I reasoned, must all be busy out the back of the store. Suddenly, a tall man in a brown overall appeared and looked me over as if I was a particularly strange species of pond life. He had unkind eyes, a sallow face, a clipped moustache and, what was most fascinating, odd, semi-inflated earlobes. He cleared his throat and asked me if I was unaccompanied. When I nodded, nervously, he turned towards the stockroom and said in his posh voice, 'I will get my assistant for you!' before promptly disappearing.

Ten or so minutes passed while I increasingly wondered if I had been forgotten about, when finally – eureka! – help appeared in the shape of a female assistant with dark, lank hair, a wart on the end of her nose and a suggestion of a moustache on her top lip (perhaps she was trying to copy her boss?). She was dressed in a slightly soiled green overall and unsmilingly introduced herself as Bella. In a stern manner she asked me what I was looking for and, a bit daunted, I squeaked out in a rush: 'A-pair-of-Stanley-Matthews-football-boots-please!' As Bella disappeared out the back, I was beginning to have real doubts about my first, solo, 'adult' shopping expedition. I had entered the shop at 9.00 a.m. sharp and here I was still, half-an-hour later, and hardly anything had happened.

As time passed, any confidence I had had was beginning to evaporate and I was just convincing myself that I should scarper (telling myself that perhaps my old play shoes would do after all), when both 'Ear Lobes' and 'Bella-with-the-wart' strode into the sales area carrying several shoeboxes – but all of them bore the Co-op logo, and with a growing dismay I could see that there was no sign of my longed-for Stanley M.

With a flourish Ear Lobes placed the stack of shoeboxes at my feet – effectively blocking me in and cutting me off from escape – and at the same time Bella, without a word, untied the laces of both of my sandshoes and removed them, before placing them out of reach on the large counter to my right. The manager then measured my foot and, nodding an 'I thought so', slipped a soccer boot he had taken from one of the Co-op shoeboxes onto my right foot. Then, smiling benignly with his (still) unkind eyes, he said proudly, 'A perfect fit!'

To my dismay, the boot now tightly fitting my foot was not the treasured brand I had asked for and, seeing my disappointment, Ear Lobes began a non-stop presentation of its better qualities: 'You can see that the "Super Co-op Hot Shot" is a far superior product than the Stanley-Whatever-Its-name is – of which we are totally out of stock anyway. Not only does the far better "Hot Shot" last and wear far longer than anything else on the market, it also has superior leather trimming and rock-hard penalty-taking toecaps. Furthermore, young sir, it only costs six shillings and threepence, making it a much cheaper buy. And,' he stressed, as if he were about to pull a rabbit out of a hat, 'you get two free tins of dubbin with every purchase!' Without pausing for breath, he then thanked me for the anticipated sale, turned towards the rear of the store and disappeared.

I looked at the vanishing back of the manger in shock. I hadn't been so astonished since the Santa Claus shambles (which was forever etched into my memory). Having not said a word, it appeared the shoe-buying decision had been made for me. Bella quickly repacked the dreaded Co-op 'Hot Shots' into their box as I sat there covered in confusion and, with an 'I'll just parcel these up for you', she headed for the stockroom.

I was totally crestfallen – what had happened? Was this how adults bought their shoes...or perhaps didn't? I couldn't quite get over the feeling that something not quite right had happened, and all the while the comments of the Mary Street gang were ringing in my ears: 'The Stanley Matthews Boot is the best in the country!', 'Philip Lynn's dad says that the wearer of the Stanley Matthews will find his game transformed overnight!' and 'The Stanley Matthews boots will guarantee an increase of goals scored – no lie!'

I found myself in a dilemma. I really wanted the Stanley Matthews football boots, but it looked like I had bought some hateful Co-op boots instead! Gulping at the thought of what my pals would say, I suddenly discovered some dormant courage and, leaping from my bamboo chair, scarpered out of the store, leaving my own shoes on the counter behind me in my panic to escape. I sprinted home shoeless and ran into the kitchen in my socks much to the astonishment of my mam, to whom I then poured out my sorry story. Handing over my dad's funds, I confessed that I didn't think I was ready yet to go solo shopping for such large items.

The next weekend my mam took me to Newcastle and there we bought a pair of treasured Stanley Matthews football boots (one size too large) and I noticed that this shoe shop took the trouble to praise my choice – no, they were not able to offer me two free tins of dubbin, but they would throw in an extra pair of football laces instead. I was over the moon. Not only was I the proud owner of a pair of Stanley Matthews football boots (and I could feel my goal-scoring abilities increasing just by holding them), but Mam had also praised me for being so forthright!

The next afternoon at our foundry field, which we called St James' Park (even though there was not a blade of grass on the surface), I played the best game of my life ever – scoring sixteen goals and captaining the winning side to victory by beating our opposition by twenty-three goals to fifteen. I never returned to the Co-op shoe shop again and I often imagined the surprised looks when 'Bella-with-the-wart' returned with the Co-op 'Hot Shots' all neatly parcelled in brown paper and string, plus the bill-of-sale made out, only to be met by a lonely pair of sandshoes and an empty shop. Some months later I was passing the store and, glancing in the window, I saw 'Bella-with-the-wart' attempting to put up a display of shoes while 'Ear Lobes' stood just behind her handing her some cartons. He still had unkind eyes and I gave a shiver, thanking my lucky stars for my narrow escape.

*   *   *

The Blaydon Co-operative Society also boasted several other different shops, including a grocery, butchers, drapery store and bakery; nearly all of these were in the main shopping area of Blaydon, but the bakery was at the edge of the town centre in a large building at the bottom of Mary Street. This building also housed the Pavilion cinema, the Co-op library, a reading room and a small (two-table) billiards room, which was one of the bases for the local billiards club.

Sometimes I was sent on an errand to the Co-op bakery shop for a granny loaf and, after the war, their delicious shortbread cakes and Danish pastries. The bakery was run with military precision by two tubby, blonde spinsters – twin sisters known locally as the Reay Girls – who lived at the bottom of Blaydon Bank with their brother Mr Reay (a familiar face as he sang alongside me in the church choir).

Although identical twins, it was quite easy to spot the difference between the two: 'Bossy', as we christened her, was aggressive, sharp-tongued and in charge. Always smart, Bossy worked behind the serving counter with great speed and was not shy in criticising those customers who were in two minds over their order. 'Dizzy', her twin, was the complete opposite – a gentle lady, she was always smiling and continually humming her favourite tune, 'Red Sails in the Sunset'. Dizzy was always covered in flour by the end of each day, unlike her sister seemed to attract streaks of jam, smears of cream and dark chocolate.

Whenever I found myself in the bakery queue I would jockey for position, even dropping back a place, so that by the time my turn came I would be served by the nicer Dizzy, who, when her sister was not looking, would sometimes slip me a free jam tart into the paper bag. Indeed, such was her generosity that I always made sure that I called on her house during Christmas week to sing my festive carols!

The large Co-op bakery, however, not only sold bread and cakes, it also had a small backroom café, where local ladies frequently had tea. I would often peer inside the entrance door of the café when I went past to see the carpeted floor and individual tables covered in white linen, which seemed to me to be in another world; totally different to the patterned oil-skin covering of our dining table standing on the bare linoleum floor of number 27 Mary Street.

I was really envious of one of my pals – Billy Clarke – whose mam had taken him to have lunch at the Co-op café for his eleventh birthday. I had always wanted to eat in the café but had never been able to persuade my mam to take me. Billy told me that the choice of menu included Spam, salad and chips, but he also said that the actual portions of food served were so small that he had left the café quite hungry!

The 28th August 1946 was my twelfth birthday and, following much concerted pestering, I finally persuaded Mam to fund a birthday lunch for me at the Co-op café – something I had desired almost as much as I had my Stanley Matthews boots! However my mam had also planned a shopping trip in Newcastle with my aunty Olive at the same time, so she asked me how would I feel if I visited the café on my own. Seeing this as a chance to have my first solo restaurant experience, I pocketed the shilling coin happily enough and set off down Mary Street, going by way of the vicarage garden before entering the bakery shop with the café at its rear.

When I arrived, the room was quite crowded and most of the tables appeared to be full. I was greeted by a young waitress called Audrey, a lovely ginger-headed girl with freckles, who showed me to a small, single table next to the window and gave me a little white card with 'Menu' typed in bold lettering at the top. Despite being the only child in a room full of chattering ladies and the odd travelling salesman reading his newspaper, I did not feel out of place. Looking over the menu, I could see that for lunch that day I could have either tripe and onions or – as I had anticipated – Spam, salad and chips. The pudding was my favourite: Spotted Dick and custard. Uppermost in my mind however was Billy Clarke's comment about very small portions.

Deciding what to order, I was thinking about the film I had seen the previous weekend at the Empire Cinema, where I had rolled with laughter at the antics of Laurel and Hardy in a posh Hollywood restaurant. I had nearly fallen off my seat I had been laughing so much at Stan Laurel, who had hidden a large caterpillar under the final piece of lettuce on his plate, having first demolished a large meal. Calling the waiter over, the comic actor had then expressed his indignation at the lack of hygiene in the restaurant and was promptly served an additional free meal. Of course Oliver Hardy could only tut, tut, and roll his eyes at his pal's boldness and cunning!

So with this in mind, I soon made my meal choice and ordered when Audrey returned to my table, acting as if I ordered such meals all the time. When my plate was served I could see that Billy Clarke was right! In front of me was a small meal consisting of a Spam, salad and only seven chips, along with a measly slice of bread and margarine and a small pot of tea. I soon set about clearing my plate and, inspired by the Laurel and Hardy film, ate everything except for one large lettuce leaf, which I left marooned (in the manner of Stan Laurel) in the centre of the plate.

Timing my cunning move, I was then able to slip a matchbox from my pocket and take from it a small caterpillar (which I had captured from the vicarage garden earlier). I then placed it unobserved under the single remaining lettuce leaf. When Audrey returned to my table, I pointed my finger towards the centre of the plate and innocently exclaimed – with my best Stan Laurel acting skills – that an intruder had reluctantly forced me to abort my meal and what would the Co-op do about it?

Holding my breath, I waited as the surprised waitress slowly lifted the salad leaf, arched her left eyebrow and pursed her lips. She quickly covered the plate with a large serviette and, placing a finger to her mouth followed by a wink, retreated from the room and into the café's kitchen at the rear. Ten minutes passed and then Audrey swept back into the room bearing a tray containing a fresh plate of Spam, salad and chips of dramatic proportions. She placed the plate in front of me with a flourish, and I ploughed through my second lunch with glee. It had worked!

When Mam arrived home from her shopping expedition, I told her about the Laurel and Hardy cunning plan I had carried out. However, instead of joining in with my pleasure at the success of my ruse, she severely ticked me off for being dishonest and sent me to bed early that evening without any supper – not that I was at all hungry! Meanwhile I related my Laurel and Hardy clever trick to the majority of the Mary Street gang, who fully appreciated the cunning of my escapade.

Indeed, later the following week, Philip Lynn tried to copy my success. However, he had the bad luck to be spotted when he released the caterpillar from his matchbox by the eagle eye of Bossy, who was giving Audrey a helping hand during a busy lunchtime. Philip was then duly banned from both the bakery shop and the café, and as a result the caterpillar plot became history.

*   *   *

During the winter months, the Blaydon billiards club was regularly held in the same building as the Co-op bakery and became one of my favourite haunts. Sometimes I would slip into the club and sit on the wooden slatted benches, watching spellbound as the members performed with great skill on the green baize. This was a world of hushed concentration and huge competitiveness and its intentness deeply impressed me.

The majority of spectators who thronged the popular venue in the winter were easily recognizable by their everyday dress of bleached powder-blue denim jackets and trousers. Throughout the warmer months of spring and summer this same group met in the large summerhouse in the Dene, just farther up from the Society building. All the members were retired employees of the LNER railway company, and I thought that on retiring, as well as being given the traditional mantelpiece clock as a retirement present, they must have also been allowed to keep their official uniforms too.

Mr Richardson, who lived across the road from my house, was one of these members and a retired steam-engine driver. He used to tell me exciting stories about his adventures on his long journeys in these snorting, awe-inspiring monsters. Little did I realize as I listened in awe to his fantastic stories, that Driver Richardson was the town's spinner of tales and fantasy! Drinking a glass of his nostril-fizzing, homemade ginger beer in his backyard and surrounded by the tobacco clouds coming from his trusty clay pipe, I would sit enthralled as he told me of his adventures.

One story involved him going on a hazardous goods-train journey from Newcastle to Bellingham during a severe Arctic winter. The normal time for the round trip, he explained, would have been about three-to-four hours, but the steam engine he was driving that day was on its last legs (having been destined for the scrap-yard the previous year, but kept in service because of the country's on-going war needs).

I listened to his tale, mouth wide open and believing every word he said, so convincing was his storytelling. He vividly described the difficult journey: how his puffing engine was constantly running out of steam through a faulty steam boiler, which had to be topped up with snow from the surrounding drifts every few miles; how he had to dig the engine out of mountainous snow drifts one hundred feet high; how he had to kill a whole sheep and barbecue it on the engine's coal fire, so that he, his fireman and the goods-train's rear guardsman could survive the journey.

He also told me how the train had been attacked by a German bomber, and how he had had to drive his train at speed into a large snowdrift to create a natural tunnel and escape the second bomb-run of the enemy! Eventually, after much toil and difficulty, he told me how they had returned to the sheds in Blaydon, having battled the elements the whole journey long, arriving some two days late!

I totally believed in Mr Richardson's stories, and the old man, who was by now in full flow, took a swig of his homemade ginger beer, and with great enjoyment told me and several of my Mary Street gang pals, who had by this time wandered into his backyard – to sit in a circle around him. My pals had arrived looking for me so that we could play another one of our marathon Test Matches in Mary Street. These matches involved using the base of a lamppost as a wicket, Dickie Hudson's old tennis ball and my own cricket bat (made from an old table leg by my dad). The last Test Match we had played had lasted some four hours, with Billie Hutchinson scoring one thousand not out! His record innings had been assisted by the downwards position of the wicket and the steeply sloped Mary Street outfield, where a well hit cover drive could elude the ring of fielders and bounce far down into the town below! In fact, during his marathon innings, Billie Hutchinson had managed to score fifty-three runs from one well-executed shot alone!

Anyway, Mr Richardson's stories had us delaying our cricket game. With a wink and a stretching of legs, he topped up his clay pipe with another supply of 'baccy' and then started to tell his now larger audience of the frightening tale of the Blaydon Lop (nit)...

Many, many years ago, he told us, the town of Blaydon had been the focus of the whole country's attention because of the humble Blaydon Lop, which, he added, had been plaguing the heads of our ancestors for centuries. (At this we all nodded in agreement, for only the other week, my mam had eye-wateringly combed both mine and my sister's heads with a fine, sharp-toothed comb, in an attempt to rid us of these annoying nits.) Our storyteller then said that, a hundred or so years ago, far away in the Chinese port of Shanghai, the local people there had also suffered from a plague of Lops, called the 'Asian Nit'. Unlike our standard Blaydon Lop, however, the Chinese 'head-jumper' was more fierce, being almost three times larger.

At this point, Philip Lynn began to scratch his head, triggering the rest of us to also begin scratching our own heads – perhaps in sympathy? 'Mr Richison,' he said, 'can you look at me heed? Cause aah think aah must 'ave cought one of those giant Chinese Lops. Aah can feel it runnin' doon me neck!'

With that our storyteller leaned across and, with a flourish, plucked a ladybird from his collar. Giving him a stern glance and a 'Yer daft bugga!', he told Philip off for interrupting his tale.

'Noo, to continue, if I may?' he said with a severe look, gathering our full attention. 'This 'ere nit was a new breed of cannibalistic nit, devourin' all other nits it could come across.' He told us that the Chinese Lop had astonished the Chinese people by growing bigger and bigger over the years – we all shuddered! – and led to most of the locals shaving their heads to avoid its assault.

Meanwhile, back in Blaydon, Mr Richardson continued, the local nit had become like a plague and had begun to make life terrible for the locals, so much so that anyone living outside the town area had stopped travelling into Blaydon at all! A reward had been offered to anyone who could rid the town of this nasty nit, which seemed to infect everyone, but especially ginger-headed people, of which there were many. At this, everyone looked straight at Billie Hutchinson, who had a mass of untidy, curly, ginger hair, and we all began to edge away from him.

Many people tried desperately to come up with different head potion formulas, Mr R continued, even telling the locals to beat each other over the head with nettle leaves! However, nothing worked. However, during this time, a Chinese cargo ship (the *Itchy Poo Tong*) happened to dock near Blaydon at Stella Staithes. As the ship docked, it inadvertently released a stowaway. At this our storyteller paused and looked each of us in the eye and asked us if we could guess what it was. We each shook our heads, mystified. Taking a puff on his pipe, he said, 'Wee', aah'll tell ye, it was the dreaded Shanghai monster Lop!'

We all gasped, and listened in horror – repeatedly scratching our heads – as Mr Richardson carried on. He told us that the monster Lop immediately jumped off the ship and galloped down along the towpath by the side of the river, arriving in town tired but really hungry. It then set about feasting on the local Blaydon Lops and within only a few hours they had all disappeared from the town, never to return in such large numbers again! (We all cheered).

Our storyteller puffed on his pipe fiercely, happy at our reaction. Then, taking a deep breath, he added that all the folk of Blaydon were so joyful at the death of their local nits that they held a festival, called 'The

Hoppings'. In the meantime, he said, the Asian nit, now full after hours of munching the plague of local head-jumpers, had by now grown to twice its normal size. Then, just as it was waddling across the main road, it was squashed by a passing horse and cart! Lying twitching on the ground, it was overheard to sigh in a strange tongue: '*Wor chu khan wor der tien ju jai sel doong mit der liem tien!*'[1] before kicking its powerful legs skywards and dying (we all cheered once more).

Alan Dodds then put his hand up and asked, 'Hoo is it Mista Richison, that you can speak Chinese, an' what does it mean?'

'Whey!' he responded, 'afore aah was an engin' drivor, aah surved me time in the Murchant Navy and visited China many, many times and picked up the lingo. An' when you get a bit oulder, aal tel ye then!' We all looked very impressed at this.

Mr Richardson then got up from his yard stool, knocking the remains of the ashes from his clay pipe, and announced that it was time for his afternoon nap. We all clapped heartily as he disappeared inside his house and then left his backyard in single file to play cricket for the rest of the day. And we all gave Billie'Ginger' Hutchinson a wide berth – just in case!

It always seemed strange to me, after hearing this story, that the local billiards club was known as 'The Lop' and I wondered if the two were connected. Still, the billiards club's general dirtiness was enough reason for the nickname, but despite this it was still very popular with older people and those out of work, who took refuge in its free warmth and shelter all day and evening long.

[1] "I go and see my god who lives in little creatures' blue heaven."

A visitor entering the billiards club would always be met by a veritable fog of pipe and cigarette fumes, and I found that when I went there I often needed several minutes to adjust to the swirling gloom before I could pick out the players, who of course had the benefit of the bright arc lights over each billiard table. The manager of the billiards room was called Joe, and, having worked for many years in the windowless room, he seemed to have altered into a hunched, pasty white gnome. He was a gentle man, but I never saw him smile and every movement he made seemed to be an effort – even resetting the snooker balls for the next game caused him to breath heavily.

The permanent cloud of tobacco smoke that hung in the air was also continually added to by Joe, who was never ever seen without a 'Tab' (cigarette) stuck in a small groove in his lower lip. This would remain in place even during a conversation, defying gravity! Because of his ever-present Tab, Joe's waistcoat lapels were always covered in tobacco ash, and it often cascaded down onto the green baize, even covering up the white lines which marked out the game on the surface of the table, much to the annoyance of the paying customers.

Apart from the gentle 'click, click' of the ivory balls, the players on the number one table played in a cathedral-like silence – especially if it happened to be a club championship final – and this was only broken as each player chalked his cue, contemplating his next strategic shot. This gap in play allowed the audience to start a short, sharp barrage of coughing and rapid clearing of throats, followed by the traditional spitting and 'pinging', as one of the spectators chewing raw tobacco directed his vile spit into one of the many copper spittoons dotted around the saw-dusted floor.

I loved slipping into the billiards club because there was always a friendly atmosphere there and it was the only place in the town centre offering a warm refuge during the day as well as the evening. However, the intense competition between players meant that sometimes tempers flared up. One evening, during the final of a club championship, Joe Walsh (the club champion) was crouching to play what would be the winning shot – a straight pot red – when the tense atmosphere was suddenly shattered by a loud, grating fart! The source of this badly timed interruption was big Jack Clasper, an ex-steam-engine fireman, who was normally a quiet and unnoticeable member.

Jack Clasper had a grey moustache under a huge, shining red nose, which was decorated with several boils. His nose was a legend among the Mary Street gang, who had all commented on it. This huge facial feature, we surmised, must be as a result of an excess of whisky and over fifty years on the trains, constantly lifting the steam engine's fire door and peering closely into the firebox to check the levels of burning fuel.

Jack's untimely eruption caused the club champion to totally miscue what would have been the final shot of the championship and allowed his opponent – Eddie Jordan – back into the match. So upset was Joe Walsh that Jack Clasper was forcibly removed from the stunned room. However, calm was restored when Eddie Jordan, in a sporting gesture, deliberately missed his next shot and so allowed the champion the chance to clinch the frame – and the match – once more.

With the championship won, the audience was free to applaud loudly and once again fill the room with a barrage of throat-clearing, spitting and the inevitable 'pinging' of the spittoons. I overheard one afternoon later that week that a sorry Jack Clasper was up in front of the billiards club committee and suspended for a week from using the club's facilities for 'unsporting' behaviour! This was a stiff penalty, but maybe well deserved, because rumour also spread at the time that he had placed a bet with the local bookie's runner on the winner of the tournament – and the bet he had placed had been on none other than Eddie Jordan!

The centrepiece of the Blaydon Co-operative Society was without a doubt the largest of its stores – the grocery shop. The Society's name was written on the outside of the shop above the large front windows in big gold letters and customers entered the store through large, highly decorated glass doors with polished brass fittings. Inside the shop were three large marble-topped counters stretching from wall to wall, and behind these was an army of white-smocked assistants, busily working away – I imagined – like clockwork soldiers.

Behind the left-hand counter, several 'infantrymen' (workers), grouped in teams of two, filled blue bags with sugar in perfect time (one assistant scooping and weighing sugar from a large hessian sack into smaller blue bags, and the other clerk expertly folding and sealing them before stacking them onto large shelves below the counter). Opposite this counter, on the other side of the shop, was a unit of troops operating a platoon of red-coloured bacon slicers. And, behind every counter there was also what seemed liked an infantry division of assistants, directly engaging with the enemy (serving the huge queue of customers).

In the centre of the shop's saw-dusted floor was a small fort (kiosk), in which sat three marooned cashier clerks, their heads just visible above the wooden sides of their tiny domain. This fort, I liked to think, was the remote headquarters for the soldiers – sending and receiving secret messages by way of small, high-flying metal canisters on an overhead, high-wire system, which linked the island fort and the counters. These whizzed and pinged at great speed across the ceiling, carrying what were in fact the payments for each customer's shopping. The high-flying canisters fascinated me every time I visited the store – they were the cleverest way of dispatching 'messages' that I knew and did not exist anywhere else in my experience.

The speed of the soldiers in the fort also impressed me, and within seconds they returned each canister to the infantry soldiers with more orders (the correct cash change, 'divi' receipt and invoice). These canisters moved along the wires at high speed by the simple pull of a lever and I often wished we had a similar system linking up all the houses of the Mary Street gang. We could easily outmanoeuver the Railway Street gang then!

My fascination of this military operation was not limited to being a spectator, however, as I was also part of the Co-op's door-to-door home-delivery grocery service. Whenever I had the chance, I was the proud assistant to Bob Embleton, the driver of the grocery horse and cart (or covered wagon as I called it). Once a week, the Co-op 'Grocery Man' Mr Holliday would visit our house on a Monday morning at 9.00 a.m. sharp to take our grocery order for a delivery later that week, something that he did for many houses in the town.

Mr Holliday would always let himself into our house by way of the unlocked backyard door, and then seat himself down at the scullery table, having the traditional cup of tea first before opening his large order book. Licking his small stub of a pencil, he would place a fresh sheet of carbon paper under a clean page of the order book and say, 'Mornin' Dot. Time is precious man, so aal just git on withit. Noo weeve got sum grand Co-op Crumpsall Cream Crackers just in – hoo aboot a cuple of packets?' and so on until he was satisfied that my mam had stretched her small weekly budget to its limit. Then he would leap up, and with a 'Must git on!' and a thank-you for the tea and the order, he would exit by way of the backyard and repeat the procedure with Mrs Nicholson, our neighbour next door.

Then, most Saturday mornings, and on many a weekday during the school holidays, I would wait outside the back entrance of the Co-op warehouse and listen for the sound of wagon wheels and the clanging and tinkling of a horse's brass adornments (the tokens from show prize medals and long service awards). I never had to wait long for the unmistakable noise of heavy clip-clopping, and this would herald the appearance of 'Tess' and her driver Bob Embleton.

Tess was a magnificent jet-black Shire horse, standing all of seventeen hands, with a flowing dark mane and an abundant covering of long hair (known as 'feathering') from the back of her knees and between her fetlocks and hooves. I grew to love this gentle and intelligent animal, and I would often admire her as I sat on the wagon which she would pull up the steep inclined cobbled stones of Blaydon Bank. On a cold winter's day, pulling a fully loaded grocery wagon and with sparks flying from her hooves, she would be like a mighty steam engine, surrounded by clouds of steam as she attempted (with snorting nostrils) to gain purchase on the shining, cobbled road surface so that she could keep up her steady pace up the steep incline.

Seated at the front of the wagon, Bob would sometimes hand the reins over to me to take control of the wagon, and I would imagine myself in Apache country, looking out for the tell-tale spiral of smoke from an Indian's secret wigwam camp. My love of these trips also lit in me a desire to have my own Shire horse when I grew up, and drive a similar wagon around. The Shire horse, I reasoned, would be easy to keep, needing only good grass and water to keep it fit and contented. It was much cheaper than the petrol-driven motorcar, which because of shortages of fuel caused by the war, was hardly seen on the roads. The Shire horse, I was sure, was here to stay for many centuries to come! If I couldn't be a steam-engine driver, then I knew one of the things that I wanted to be – a top grocery-cart driver.

Charlie Stanley was the manager of the Co-op butcher's shop, which he ran with real flair and style. He was tall and slim, and as well as his job as a butcher, every weekend he changed into the area's 'Mr Show Business' – the conductor of 'Charlie Stanley's Five-Piece, Rhythmic Dance Band'. His musical group, as he liked to call it, played every Saturday evening at the local Church Hall. Charlie's dark hair was always slicked down with lashings of brilliantine, and with his smart tuxedo he was transformed into a taller image of the Nation's most famous bandleader, Joe Loss!

* * *

Charlie Stanley's musical fame gave him (so he thought!) a VIP reputation in the town, but he was quite often laughed at by the locals, many of whom saw him as a 'bit of a Charlie!' and a 'big head', possessing 'airs and graces' above his station! I heard that he had disowned his parents, who lived in the poorer end of town in Blaydon Haughs, despite the fact that his dad was a member of the local colliery band and had introduced him to the world of music.

His bossy, 'I'm in total charge' approach from his role as a bandleader crossed over to his day-to-day role as a butcher and meant that his hardworking assistant, Dickie Hudson Senior – the dad of Dickie Hudson, fellow Apache – was always being told to do the majority of jobs around the store. However, Charlie always liked to serve each customer personally, and for his favourites he even wrapped up the meat order!

This meant that Dickie Hudson Senior still had to do every other task in the shop. Each morning he would open up the store at 8.00 a.m. sharp, before hosing down the solid wood chopping tables and struggling to transfer the huge meat carcasses from the rear freezer to the large hooks on the back wall of the shop. He also had the job of removing the previous day's blood-spattered sawdust from the shop floor and replacing it each morning with a fresh, dazzling white covering. This sawdust he collected in two large sacks from Tom Smith, the carpenter in the Co-op undertaker's (which was to be found by way of a steep flight of stairs on the outside of the tall building the butcher's was in, and next to the Co-op stables; a punishing journey). Then Dickie also had to clean all of the shop's large front windows and polish the door brass handles.

Charlie Stanley would arrive at the shop every morning at 8.55 a.m., where he would put on his pristine blue-and-white-striped overall and fancy gold armbands. After nodding his approval, somewhat majestically, to his assistant at the well-organised store, he would then unlock the front door and greet the first customers, whistling his favourite tune 'The Blue Danube' (his dance band's opening and closing signature tune).

Once, when I joined the quickly forming queue outside the Co-op's butcher's (with 'Hurry! Hurry! John! Take the basket to the Co-op – they've got sausages in!' from my mam still ringing in my ears), I overheard two women whispering in the queue in front of me that Charlie Stanley had the 'hots' (whatever that meant) for the wife of the manager of the Plaza cinema. Apparently the butcher had been spotted handing a large carrier bag to 'Dorothy Lamour' at the rear of the shop, and much was made out of what this could mean. As it turned out, the contents were for her Pekingese pet (or so she told Billy Drury's sister, who worked in the ticket box office at the Plaza cinema). However, this was not enough to stop the rumour circulating around the town that the two resident butchers – Messrs Tweddle and Stanley – were at loggerheads over the favours of the lovely Madam Lamour.

At our weekly Mary Street Apache pow-wow on Summerhill, whilst passing around our smoking peace pipe, Crazy Hands – Billie Hutchinson – claimed that he had overheard his next-door neighbour telling his mam that the whole affair was about to come to a head in Wesley Square the following Sunday at 'High Noon'! Crazy Hands added that although Gary Cooper was not going to be present, a duel was to take place with the weapons already chosen – meat cleavers! As further evidence, I could personally vouch for the weapon selection, because only the day before I had seen Master Butcher Tweddle sharpening his huge meat cleaver more vigorously than ever.

The day of the duel soon arrived and right after matins church service we tore off our cassocks and surplices and sprinted out of the vestry, heading directly for Wesley Square. When we arrived, panting and gasping, we were surprised that with the dramatic showdown about to take place, there were very few spectators to be seen. However our spirits were soon lifted when the Salvation

Army band trooped down the stairs leading from their upstairs Hall, gathered into position in the square, and started playing. Surely this was the pre-entertainment before the main event – proof that something exciting was about to take place! Why even the first hymn opened with the words 'Onward Christian soldiers, marching as to war!' – a sure sign of the battle to come.

Twenty minutes passed, and the only person to join the crowd (the Mary Street gang, a couple of old women sitting in the square, and a dog) was Alan Dodds' younger brother with his hoop and stick. There was no sign of the two duelists and their seconds. We waited and waited, until even the Salvation Army band finished playing and packed up their instruments. We finally left the square, downcast and disappointed, and wound our way slowly home for Sunday lunch. Perhaps we had got the dates mixed up?

However, the whole dramatic episode of rumour and counter-rumour came to an abrupt halt when the following month there was a change of management at the Plaza cinema. The old manager Mr Tindall left the town with his wife Dorothy Lamour, because, according to Billie's mam, Mr T had been promoted to a popular Newcastle city cinema – the Essoldo. However, not only did their departure mean that one of the favourite topics of the gossip-mongering machine of Blaydon had gone, so had my career as a sometime courier and spy. Some days later, after Madame Lamour's departure, Mr Tweddle took me aside in his store and, squeezing a sixpence into my hand, quietly informed me that in future all invoices would be sent by post. My services were no longer needed! I was a free agent once again – free, that is, to turn my mind to my next money-making scheme...

Chapter Eleven

Fun and Games in the Pew

I was recruited by the Church of England at the tender age of seven years, three months. I can clearly remember my audition with the choirmaster in the musty vestry of St Cuthbert's, surrounded by rows of dark-coloured cassocks smelling of mothballs, which hung in the open wardrobes running down along two sides of the room. There was also a jumble of white surplices thrown into a wicker basket, and the vestry was bathed in the late evening's sunshine. This streamed in through the large, ornate, stained-glass window, which looked out onto the overgrown church graveyard.

My granddad was a staunch member of the congregation and had arranged for the audition to take place one Sunday evening after evensong service. Mam waited outside the vestry door while I seated myself on one of the empty bench seats nervously waiting for the choirmaster. The only singing I had done up till then was during school assembly or joining in with the Plaza cinema's noisy Saturday morning matinee chorus with my pals (chewing on our liquorice sticks and following the words with the on-screen magic 'bouncing ball' focusing attention on the words. I was nervous about singing.

The choirmaster and organist Mr Lawton, who had a ginger snuff-tinged moustache and was forever chewing mints, started the audition by asking me my age, quickly followed by, 'Did I enjoy music?', 'Did I believe in Jesus Christ?' and 'What was my favourite hymn?' Thinking for a second, I replied, 'Seven', 'Yes', 'Yes' and '"In the Bleak Midwinter"'. After a few moments the choirmaster, tugging at his cassock, stood up and said to my complete surprise: 'Welcome, John!' and gave me a penny (perhaps a joining on fee?). He then handed me an extra strong mint, tweaked my elbow and, smiling, led me out through the vestry door to my waiting mam.

With a 'Congratulations, Mrs Solomon – John will be fine. Don't forget, choir practice is on Tuesday evenings – 6.30 sharp', he scurried back into the church, where soon the sad sound of 'Jesu, Joy of Man's Desiring' could be heard through the open vestry door.

My mam, praising me for passing the audition, said, 'I always knew you would have a good voice like our Joan's' – Joan, my sister, was a talented singer – and with that we walked up the steep street towards home and our traditional Sunday evening's supper (the remainder of that week's ration of cold lamb meat – left over from lunchtime – which thinly sliced with mint sauce made some delicious sandwiches). Happy she was pleased, I never told my mam that the choirmaster had not asked me to sing during the audition! Perhaps Mr Lawton had guessed that with my angelic face – as I was often told – I would turn out to be a good soprano!

I arrived at my first choir practice the following Tuesday evening, where there were only five other boys present and I began to suspect that my easy admission to the choir was to make up the numbers. Over the next couple of weeks the size of the choir quickly grew as I encouraged my Mary Street pals to join as well, tempting them to enlist with the signing-on fee of one penny plus the bonus of free fruit at the next church harvest festival, due in a couple of months' time. Mostly, however, the rest of the gang finally agreed to join because they wouldn't have to endure a singing audition!

Apart from its growing number of boy sopranos, the choir also had a strong team of male singers. The majority of them were tradesmen from the town, like Peter Craig (fruiterer), Big Jack 'Spokes' Percy (cycle shop) and Dickie Hudson Senior (butcher). Jack Percy had a magnificent, military-style moustache and I fantasised that because of this 'whizzo prang' RAF moustache, he was a secret part-time RAF pilot, who humbly preferred to remain anonymous with regard to his dangerous, war night-time adventures. I imagined that he successfully concealed his RAF military identity, despite the handlebar moustache, because of his cover of working in a cycle shop during the day – this meant that he was seen regularly during normal shop hours, doing various cycle chores in his store, hiding the fact that he had actually been on another one of his dangerous, night-time, Lancaster Bomber sorties across Germany the night before.

As added proof, it was true that none of my pals nor myself had ever seen Jack Percy out and about in the evening, apart from at the Sunday evensong service. I later discovered that as a trained engineer, he was closeted in his garage every spare moment of his time, carefully putting together a vintage motorcar he had found in one of Tweddle's old barns. In the meantime, some of my street pals believed my 'Bomber' theory and Jack Percy would often receive from them military-style salutes – much to his surprise – when they entered his store, or hangar as we called it!

We also liked Jack Percy because he would sometimes liven up the sermon during the Sunday evening song service, especially when it was very boring. Often, midway through the Reverend's dull preaching, and with some of the choir members nodding off, Jack would run through his repertoire of made-to-order 'wake-up' calls in the form of 'controlled' farting! Such interruptions greatly appealed to all of the Mary Street gang and we always waited for their 'appearances' eagerly. Jack's talent meant that he could make a farting noise amazingly appear to come from one of his fellow tenors, snoozing some yards farther along the hard wooden bench. This often produced a loud 'Tut, tut!'

from Deaconess Lakey, who sat in the corner pew close to the choir stalls, and an angry stare from the vicar in the pulpit. The targeted, startled male choir member would then awaken from his slumbers with a start and a sheepish and bewildered look on his face, often with spittle on his chin!

Jack Percy – or the Wing Commander as I personally called him – had the exceptional gift of being able to fart at whatever volume was needed to suit the occasion, he also possessed the power of anal ventriloquism. Rumour had it that, prior to the Sunday evening service, he would feast on nothing but sprouts, washed down with pints of dandelion and burdock! However, the main problem I had with this mid-sermon entertainment was that, on hearing one of Jack's specials, I immediately went into uncontrolled fits of laughter, which I manfully tried to stifle whilst trying not to appear as the guilty party (which I wasn't). Indeed, so bad was this that once or twice I had to dash home immediately after the church service for a much-needed change of underwear!

*   *   *

It was a bitterly cold Christmas evening when I, along with droves of fellow churchgoers, staggered and slithered down the steep incline of Mary Street towards St Cuthbert's Church. Over the past two days, Blaydon and the surrounding countryside had been hit by a ferocious Arctic storm raging in from the North Sea. The only way to get to the town centre was by narrow pathways cut through the snow by people walking in Indian file, the pearly white snow piled several feet high on either side.

Tonight was Christmas Eve and I was particularly excited, not only by the surrounding wonderful sledging conditions, but also by the fact that during the coming evening, I was going to be singing my first solo hymn in the carol service, appropriately called 'In the Bleak Midwinter'. This year had seen a change of the custodian of St Cuthbert's, with the arrival of a new rector – the Reverend H. O. Duncan – who, on taking up the leadership of his flock, and in total contrast to the previous rector, had attempted to change (in large and small ways) certain aspects of the day-to-day running of the church and the relationship between the vicar, worshipper and indeed God himself!

The introduction of rectory garden fêtes and the encouragement of live dramatised religious pageants in the Church Hall had been greeted by all as an excellent contribution towards an active and supportive growing congregation. However not everything was met with such enthusiasm. Led by the formidable Mothers' Union 'mafia' bosses – 'Nipped-In Bette' and 'Rent-a-Mouth' Mrs Brown – there began slowly to stir a restless mood throughout the older section of the congregation, many of whom, my mam said, still resented the transfer of the old rector (who had been a traditional Church of England minister) to pastures new.

The introduction of a small bit of Latin occasionally slipping into the vicar's sermons, and the Rev. Duncan's recent 'fashion' change from the standard, dark grey cassock to a gaudy purple one had already raised several eyebrows. The Mothers'

Union committee meeting (really an excuse to meet and gossip) soon began to talk about the vicar's new-fangled and odd ways, and especially how he treated his flock, rather than following the standard weekly agenda covering charitable events; who would be going to visit the sick and elderly in the Parish and so on. Indeed, recent meetings had become more and more discontented. The overall opinion was that there was a real danger that the church of St Cuthbert's was moving towards what my mam explained was a 'High Church' way of doing things and therefore – horror of all horrors – closer ties with Roman Catholicism!

This was not to be borne! Why, on several occasions had not the Rev. Duncan been spotted by two committee members in deep conversation in Wesley Square with the enemy (the local Catholic priest)? However, worse than this was what the Rev. Duncan had carried out recently one Sunday morning after the morning communion service. Rather than going straight home, I, along with the rest of the young choir members, had been invited by the vicar to go down to the rectory basement (usually used for bible-reading classes and the occasional game of table tennis) for free biscuits and lemonade. We all trooped down eagerly as this was a real bonus, though not as much of a treat for me because Dickie Hudson spilled his pop over my ration of biscuits and refused to swop.

After we had got our treat, the vicar then passed out sheets of writing paper and pencils and asked us to write down those sins we had each committed over the past week, explaining that it was good to be able to privately confess our sins and thereby cleanse our souls! We were all at a bit of a loss and quite bemused, but we did as we were instructed.

Following this odd incident, we all left the vicarage and gathered together at the bottom of Mary Street to compare our sins. Billie Hutchinson had confessed to 'stealing' some apples from Tweddle's orchard. I personally could not recall any 'sins' during the previous week, but, believing that I had better write something down, I had confessed to stealing a fig biscuit from my mam's cupboard (which in fact I hadn't). Alan Dodds said he had owned up to hiding his younger brother's top and whip, because he wouldn't to share it with him. Philip Lynn, however, had misunderstood the whole exercise and, believing that he was meant to write about the best lie that he could think of, had promptly written: 'Set fire to Tweddle's farmhouse and stole his sheep!'

At home, when I told Mam about the pop-and-biscuit session, she was furious. She stormed off up the bank to Polmaise Street – the unofficial Mothers' Union 'mafia' headquarters and the home of Aunty "'Nipped-In' Bette" – to relate this latest, awful Popish behaviour!

So, the inevitable showdown took place on that wintry Christmas Eve. Every pew was full of worshippers – the back of the church packed with late arrivals dressed in their winter clothing, and the men, having removed their caps and balaclavas, stamping their feet on the cold, stone slab floor and rubbing their hands together to keep their circulation going, despite the presence of the heated church radiators. The carol service soon started and it was not long before I was on my feet to sing my carol solo. I loved the experience – standing in front of the large congregation and being able to hold every top note. In between verses, I glanced down towards the pews and saw my mam with a broad smile on her face, offering supportive encouragement.

As I sat down, my solo turn over, I noticed that the church had suddenly become very warm. Perhaps it was my imagination, but there also seemed to be a hint of white smoke swirling around the pulpit area and the entrance door to the vestry. It was now time for the usual evening sermon and the Rev. H. O. Duncan slowly climbed the pulpit stairs, unfolded his notes and began: 'In the name of the Father and of—' but got no farther!

Suddenly standing up from their front pew and brandishing their prayer books, the local Mothers' Union confronted the vicar. Led by the staunch Mrs Brown, and firmly supported by 'Nipped-In', they rang a peal down over the helpless Rev. Duncan – 'Whey! Are ye still not satisfied with yer Papist ways? Noo, for aall to see, another example of yer high-filuting pagan beliefs! Ye're not content to bribe wore innocent children to confessions – here, for everyone to see, is the last bloody' – (gasp from the congregation) – 'straw! INCENSE! ROMAN CATHOLIC INCENSE!' Mrs Brown shrieked and pointed to the slight swirl of smoke hovering over the pulpit.

The congregation were horrified and several elderly members obviously in sympathy left their pews and began to exit the church. They were then followed by the Mothers' Union leaders, still brandishing their prayer books, having been shepherded out of the building by three sombre-looking sidesmen (who usually only had to take around the collection box). The Rev. H. O. Duncan bravely tried to carry on with his sermon, somewhat subdued and upset, explaining to the remaining stunned flock that the white mist surrounding the pulpit was as much a mystery to him as to everyone else.

Once the service was over, Matty Dixon (the verger) inspected the nearby radiators and the church boiler room to discover that the culprit 'incense' was not the addition of more Popish ways, as the vicar had been accused of, but the leakage of steam from a nearby pulpit radiator! The caretaker, anticipating a 'full house' that festive evening, had stoked up the steam-driven boiler to its maximum pressure. This, combined with the fast dropping evening temperatures, had then caused one or two of the rusty church radiator valves to pop and release a small amount of steam.

Some weeks later, 'Nipped-In' and 'Motor Mouth' slipped back into the bosom of the all-forgiving church and made their peace with the Rev. Duncan – presumably they had 'confessed' to their misunderstanding of the incense incident; however I don't know if they were asked to write down their confession on a sheet of paper during their meeting in the rectory as well!

Chapter Twelve

St James' Park

Just before I reached my twelfth birthday, my dad introduced me to the exciting world of the football supporter by taking me to my first professional match at St James' Park to support that famous north-east soccer team – Newcastle United. That day the match was Newcastle United versus Portsmouth, and I was captivated! The war was over and there were no more air raids, so the resumption of league football had allowed the local working-class men to be able to at last look forward to their Saturday afternoons' entertainment. Like my dad, I became a true Geordie fan, and along with thousands of others, was in the pits of hell or the heights of heaven every weekend, depending on the final score of the match.

On this day, there were over fifty thousand supporters at the match and my dad – an enthusiastic supporter and a more than useful outside left for our top local amateur team, Spen Black and Whites – hoisted me up onto his broad shoulders in the Gallowgate end of the ground, giving me my first clear view of the most amazing battle of skill I had ever seen. However, on this particular trip to the football, for me and the thousands of other supporters, there was to be heartbreak and disappointment – the Magpies, as they were nicknamed, lost a very competitive game.

Though I was part of an extremely supportive crowd, I noticed that each time the Portsmouth's outside right – Harris – received the ball there was an instance of hush and a collective intake of breath around me. Apart from being small in size and having a very large nose, his ball control was brilliant and he possessed amazing speed. He mesmerised the home defence and, indeed, scored the winning goal, with Portsmouth victorious by two goals to one. As we drifted home from the ground and made our way to the tram stop next to the central station, the surrounding chat was not of Messrs Milburn, Walker and co. but was a sporting collective admission that the man of the match could only be 'That buggar Harris!'

Despite the Magpies losing, I was hooked and I soon began to travel to Newcastle for every home game and the few reserve matches. I often went with my Mary Street pals, complete with my black and white scarf (knitted by my aunty Nancy) and my trusty wooden corncrake rattle. On our visits, we soon realized that it was important to arrive at the grounds well before the kick-off time at 2.30 p.m. to get ahead of the main wild supporters' rush. So, we always arrived outside the grounds in good time, armed with our carrier bags containing our various supplies – my lunchtime snack often repeating the previous evening's dinner menu – such as cold rice pudding sandwiches, an apple and a slice of homemade fruit tart.

My pals and I always joined the queue, which began to form around 11.00 a.m., at the 'boys' turnstile gate entrance, which opened at 1.00 p.m. sharp. The match admission was 9d, which I carefully guarded all the way to the grounds. By arriving early, not only were we always near the head of the queue, we were also able to claim a coveted place in the stadium seated at the front of the stands on the low wall running around outside the edge of the pitch – something that gave us an unbroken view of the game.

Before the kick-off, we would be treated to some wonderful pre-game entertainment, a regimented military or local colliery brass band often blasting out musical tunes whilst strutting up and down the pitch. We also joined in the roars of laughter and cheers as we watched the incredible – and quite daunting – sight of young lads, who had arrived too late to grab a front pitch-side position, attempt to get a better place in the front (where they would be able to see the game instead of being stuck at the back behind a huge wall of adult spectators). These lads would bravely run the gauntlet of being tossed physically above the heads of the sloping crowd down towards the pitch, and often their flying momentum – bouncing at a great height – generated a massive roar from the spellbound crowd. Flying like human missiles, they would often come crashing down onto the head of some unsuspecting spectator eating his pie, unaware that he was providing the cushioning for the boy's fall!

However, the most enjoyable pre-match entertainment came from watching the white-jacketed ice-cream sellers, most of whom were university students earning some extra pocket money. (Ice cream was a real treat, and had only become available again just after the war had ended. The Empire cinema had been the first to pull off a real coup in this regard as they were the first cinema in the area to offer ice-cream choc bars to its filmgoers. One early evening, I had been trudging home past the Empire cinema from the nearby town railway station – where I had been train-spotting – when I heard a loud 'Pisst!' from the front box office. My aunty Hannah worked in the ticket kiosk there – she was my father's cousin, a lovely woman who was plump, had a whorl eye and early greying hair. I dashed up the cinema steps to the kiosk and Aunty Hannah, with a furtive glance around, slipped me a small, brown paper bag. 'Nee money,' she whispered. 'Noo hadaway and diffin't tell anybody!' she added and dismissed me with a conspiratorial wink. Glancing inside the bag, I couldn't have been more surprised if it had been filled with gold. Inside there was the unlikely sight of an Eldorado ice-cream choc bar in a foil wrapper! I gave a gasp of delight. I hadn't had such a treat for several years! I quickly sprinted home and breathlessly handed over the prize item to my mam. With whoops of joy, we shared the tiny ice cream with my sister, and I even licked out the wrapper just so as I could get every last bit of ice cream taste there was.)

Anyway, at the football ground, the ice-cream sellers would parade their precious wares in handheld trays around the outside of the pitch. These sellers had to be able to successfully deliver their ice-cream bars to the eager buyers standing in the crowd and then take their money, all without leaving their positions. I could see that there was a lot of skill involved in this, which mainly required the art of accurate throwing, something which Billie Hutchinson told me was rigorously practised by students who wanted become these ice-cream sellers

He said that a friend of his elder sister – a student at King's College London – had had to practise for many hours before going to a job interview with the ice-cream company. I was very much impressed when I heard that this fellow had practised throwing an object accurately into large empty boxes placed at different distances for many hours. At the job interview, he had had to show off his ability in a test run set up just for the occasion. Only by being able to prove he could successfully throw several missiles in a row to different locations was he then offered the weekend job!

It was usually about an hour before the start of each match when these specially trained ice-cream sellers would appear. Spectators who wanted an ice-cream bar would raise their arms and this sign the sellers quickly saw and answered, no matter where the customer happened to be in the crowd, whether it was near the front, the middle or at the rear. Then the customer would throw their shilling coin down over the wall of his fellow spectators towards the hallowed turf below, and in return (and this was the tricky bit!), and trusting in the accuracy of the ice-cream seller's throwing arm, he was expected to catch the iced missile hurled high into the air in his direction. Amazingly, most of the ice-cream bars seemed to reach their destinations, but sometimes the choc ice would part company with its wrapper whilst still in the air and would then unfortunately land short of its target, splattering onto the head of some unsuspecting fellow supporter below – an event that was followed by roars of laughter around the ground.

All first-team matches were supported by a fanatical crowd, often overstretching the ground's official capacity of sixty thousand. This would result in surges in different areas of the stands as latecomers straight from the nearby pubs (many the worse for wear) pushed spectators from the rear and caused an alarming, downward ripple effect. Such surges often led to the crowd over-spilling onto the edge of the pitch, and this would hold up the match starting, much to the annoyance of everyone else in the crowd, me and my pals included. Still, this was never enough to put us off – it was just all part of the game!

So, every match day we would eagerly set off from home and walk the few miles to the village of Scotswood, across the Chain bridge and over the coaly River Tyne to board a tramcar bound for the city. Although there was a frequent bus service from Blaydon to Newcastle, by walking those few miles and catching the cheaper tram, we could save some of our money and have the luxury of spending the fare difference on extra liquorice sticks or a ripe calabash pear from the street traders outside the football ground.

My pals and I went to many exciting games, but the most thrilling and dramatic one was the FA Cup tie, where we played the dangerous team of Bolton Wanderers. To our dismay, the 'Geordies' were two–nil down against formidable opponents, captained by the renowned international centre-forward Nat Lofthouse.

The Gallowgate flag had just been lowered, signalling that less than ten minutes of playing time was remaining, when, out of the blue, centre forward Jackie Milburn scored with a scorching drive from about twenty-five yards. Perhaps there was just a chance to equalize and gain a replay? With an amazing roar, St James' Park ignited with 'Gan on the lads!', followed by a heady rolling chorus of the Geordie national anthem: 'The Blaydon Races', which I joined in with great pride as a Blaydon lad.

The match was transformed as we sang at the top of our lungs! The Geordies launched attack after attack, totally taking over the game, but with only five minutes remaining, would they, could they somehow score the all-important equalizing goal? Bobby Mitchell, our Scottish international left-wing pied-piper (who despite undoubted and mesmerising ball skills irritated the home supporters by his often selfish play), received the ball on the halfway line and set off on one of his typical mazy runs. Despite the baying from the frenzied spectators imploring him to release the ball – perhaps a through pass to Milburn? – he continued his run at the Bolton defence.

With the Bolton rearguard expecting him to release the ball at any time, they slowly backed off, continuing to mark the other Newcastle forwards – but Bobby just kept on advancing! Suddenly he had penetrated the opponents' penalty area and, with a quick look up, planted a delicious chip over the goalkeeper's head! Two–Two! The crowd went wild. Then amazingly, with seconds to go, 'Wor Jackie Milburn' also scored with a pile-driver of a goal just outside the penalty box: Three–Two!

The final whistle blew, ending the most thrilling game I had ever seen. The crowd around me was madness – grown men, complete strangers, surrounded me, hugging and embracing each other. Like me, they were overwhelmed with the excitement and many cried tears of joy. That day, most of us were unable to speak on the tram journey home – we had become hoarse with all of the shouting and screaming. What a game! What a result!

Such excitement and drama meant that on the way home I turned my thoughts to how I could join the ranks of professional footballers, who were rumoured to receive at least five pounds per week – an enormous sum. Plus, the thrill of playing in front of thousands of spectators and the joy of being constantly recognised and stopped for autographs whilst walking down the city streets was very appealing.

Forget being an International Courier Spy or a steam-train engine driver, what I was going to be was a Newcastle United footballer! Immediately on arriving home that late afternoon, I began to practise in my exercise book the style of my personal autograph. Tomorrow I decided I would be down to the foundry field straight after breakfast with my Mary Street pals in tow, to improve my passing skills and practise some delicious chips over the goalkeeper. I was on my way!

Epilogue

The Future Trail?

One glorious spring afternoon after Sunday School, I made my way to Stella Woods to check on a pheasant's nest I had discovered the weekend before, nestling under an old haystack in the corner of a field next to Stoney's pond. As befitting an Apache Brave, I stealthily approached the nest in a crouched position, carefully checking the surroundings to see that I was not being watched by any bird's-nesting rival. Then, satisfied that this was not so, I got nearer to the nest, accidentally disturbing the hen bird sitting there. She immediately gave out an indignant squawk before flying away with several more guttural cries, to warn any of its pals that there was an intruder among them.

To my delight and astonishment, I saw that the three beautiful brown eggs I had seen there the previous week had been joined by a further eight. Taking just the one egg for my collection, I ran to a nearby hawthorn hedge and plucked out a thorn to puncture the top and bottom of the egg with. Then I gently blew out the contents of the egg and slipped the fragile shell into my trusty, cotton-wool-lined, tin snuffbox, which was hanging by a string around my neck.

Glowing with my success – this find was the largest single nest of eggs I had ever seen – I slowly made my way down into the woods to my secret den next to my huge guardian hazel tree, 'Goliath'. As I sat on the grassy bank by the stream, I could hear the song of a nearby thrush; its beautiful sound, I thought, must surely make all the other birds feel jealous.

Throwing a twig into the water, I watched it spin and float away and I wondered where it would eventually end up. Then I pondered what future destination beckoned for me in that great stream of life, not only for myself but also for my brave Apache brothers. Certainly over the last few years or so, I had considered many future jobs for when I grew up – from International Courier Spy or Spitfire pilot to professional footballer or steam-engine driver. Or perhaps, I thought, I could be like Peter Pan and I would never grow up, being able to carry on my wonderful life of fun, freedom and laughter for ever. Certainly the difficulties of the war, like rationing and the blackout, had not affected my life as much as others. Apart from being hungry for most of the time, I had seen the war as exciting and a real adventure.

Now, the war was over and sitting alone in my den on the bank of the stream, I realised how lucky I had been with my family and pals; that whatever happened to me in the future, nothing could ever replace the lively, day-to-day adventures of my childhood. The past few years had been unforgettable, from dashing through meadows and cornfields, helping to stook the corn sheaves in the field, to sitting exhausted at the rear of a horse-driven hay cart as it made its way back to the farmyard. From the pleasures of fishing with a branch or eating wild fruit, pignuts and sucking on stalks of wild fennel, to the enjoyment of drinking cool sparkling water from covert springs and cooling my feet in the icy stream on a hot summer's day. And especially, from the fun and games with brave fellow Apaches to the satisfaction of trudging home with my legs and arms scratched from that day's bird's-nesting or blackberry picking.

Lengthening shadows and the sparkling late evening dew brought me back to the present. Dusk was coming and I got up to follow my homeward trail, now and then lit by the deepening, blood-red sunset. In the fading light, I could hear the 'towoo-towoo' of a barn owl, and I broke easily into a trot to get home to my supper and my safe, comfy bed. The future spread ahead of me full of hope. Many times at our regular pow-wows on Summerhill, my brave Apache brothers had talked about what they might be when they grew up – Brave Buffalo (Philip Lynn) had said he would be a bank robber; Black Hawk (me) had finally chosen the life of a professional footballer; Crazy Hands (Billie Hutchinson) wanted to be a Spitfire pilot; Running

Brave (Alan Dodds) said he would be a submarine captain; Chief Brown Legs (Dickie Hudson) had said he was going to be an Olympic champion and, finally, Big Wigwam Callaghan (Fatty Callaghan), well, he said he was going to be a famous Sumo wrestler! Looking forward to being home, somehow I knew that all of these were possible.

*   *   *

Autumn, 2007:

I often wonder whatever happened to my brave Apache pals. Did they ignore their original aspirations and develop into true Apache warriors? I guess some of them are now, in all probability, dancing a celebratory, ritual 'fertility dance' in that great reservation in the sky. Or with good luck and health, some may have withstood the onslaught of years and are now sitting contentedly in their mortgage-free wigwams. Still, wherever they are, I know that a part of me is still with them in spirit, at one long pow-wow on Summerhill, re-tipping our arrows and enjoying an endless smoke of our cinnamon-filled peace pipe

Also by John Solomon

Soapy Business

Soapy Business takes you back to the 1950s before supermakets and identikit town centres. Shops were family owned by 'idiosyncratic retail management style'. John reveals the cut-and-thrust world of the soap salesman – with on-going tussels with grocers and devious methods of beating his competitors. 'Suds Law' if things could go wrong they often did.

A burgeoning career with a higly desirable company car created many opportunities for an eager, single young man coming-of-age.

A charming and light-hearted read, full of warmth and optimism. John Solomon's entertaining and amusing confessions of a soap salesman evoke the spirit of a by-gone era. A delight – and a dose of laughter to banish those washday blues!

1-903506-14-x £7.99

Other books from Zymurgy

We Never Had It So Good

By David Williams

A book about childhood and growing-up in a northern mining town. It is set in the late 1950s, when children were free spirited 'adventurers', roaming the streets and making their own entertainment. Bonfire night, the miners' gala, leek competitions, the annual fair and school life all feature in this gritty and entertaining collection of short stories.

It is a book that will appeal to all readers of John Solomon's titles: nostalgic, amusing and set in the north of east of England.

978-1903506-28-8 £7.99

Natural North

by Allan Potts
Foreword by the Duke of Northumberland

A photographic celebration of flora and fauna in the North of England. Supporting text provides background information. Sections cover; high fells, upland, woodland, agricultural, coastal and urban areas.

ISBN 1 903506 00X hb 160pp £16.99

Bent Not Broken

by Lauren Roche

Lauren Roche's autobiography; an abused child, stowaway, stripper, prostitute, drug abuser. She turned her life around to become a doctor. An international best seller. Lauren has been interviewed by Lorraine Kelly, Esther Rantzen, Johnny Walker, Simon Mayo and others.

ISBN 1 903506 026 pb 272pp + 8pp plate section £6.99

A Lang Way To The Pawnshop

by Thomas Callaghan
Introduction by Sid Chaplin

An autobiographical account of growing up in 1930s urban Britain; a family of ten, two bedrooms, no wage earner. An amusing insight into a period of history still in living memory.

ISBN 1 903506 018 pb 144pp £6.99

The Krays: The Geordie Connection
by Steve Wraith and Stuart Wheatman
Foreword by Dave Courtney

After seeing the Krays at a funeral on the news (aged ten) Steve writes letters, meets the brothers and eventually becomes one of 'the chaps'. The book is about the Krays final years and how they ran things on the outside.

ISBN 1 903506 042 pb 240pp + 8pp plate section £6.99

The River Tyne From Sea to Source

by Ron Thornton
Foreword by Robson Green

A collection of nearly eighty water colours and hundreds of pencil drawings following the River Tyne from outside the harbour to the source of the North and South Tyne rivers. Supporting text provides a wealth of information on the history surrounding the Tyne.

ISBN 1 903506 034 hb 160pp £16.99

Life On The Line

by Lauren Roche

Following on from Bent Not Broken the book covers Lauren's life once she becomes a doctor. Bankruptcy, depression, a suicide attempt - and the shock revelation that her son was a sex offender. What can a mother do when she suspects that one of her children is being abused? What happens when you discover that the abused child has become an abuser?

ISBN 1 903506 050 pb 192pp + 8pp plate section £6.99

A Memoir of The Spanish Civil War

by George Wheeler
Foreword by Jack Jones
Edited by David Leach

Thousands from across the world went to Spain to form the International Brigades; many did not return. Through George Wheeler's experience and memories of the Spanish Civil War you will discover what the war was really like. What were they fighing for? Why did the Spanish people fail in their fight against facism?

1 903506 077 pb 192pp + 8pp plate section £8.99

Alcatraz Island Memoirs of a Rock Doc

by Milton Daniel Beacher, M.D
Edited by Dianne Beacher Perfit

MiltonDaniel Beacher, M.D. arrived on Alcatraz Island a naive and compassionate young doctor. One year later he left with a journal.It chronicled the suicides, discipline problems, force feedings , and details of a long strike and successful escape.

He also penned conversations with famous prisoners like Al Capone, Alvin Karpis and Machine Gun Kelly. Dr Beacher later worve the journal into a vivid acoount of life on the Rock.

1 903506 085 pb 240 pp + 8pp plate section £6.99

Back Lanes and Muddy Pitches

by Robert Rowell

A book about playing football and growing up. Robert Rowell's football career starts within earshot and eyesight of mum; with lamp posts for floodlights and garage doors for goals. When he gets older matches are played in the park with jumpers for goalposts. Robert gets the ultimate call-up, a place in the school team. After leaving school, student life, then the joys of starting work. The book follows Robert's life through football to middle–age.

A book for everyone who enjoys football and reading.

ISBN 1 9103506 12 3 pb 288 pp £6.99

Willi Whizkas
– Tall Tales and Lost Lives!
by Paws and Claws

Willi Whizkas is an ordinary cat who shares his home with two humans. He is fed up with the same cat food every day, envious of his friends – they all have cat flaps and he hates the vet.

His life is far from humdrum and routine. He has a great set of friends, loves exploring and having adventures.

A must read for all cat lovers.

ISBN 1 903506 18 2 pb 256 pp £7.99

Northstars

by Sid Smith, Chris Phipps and John Tobler

A celebration of musicians with north–eastern roots, based on exclusive interviews from Royal Television Society award winning TyneTees series of the same name. The book honours the role of north-east musicians in the history of popular music.

From rock 'n' roll to heavy rock, pop to punk, electonic to acoustic folk, Northstars documents how musicians from the region have made it to the world stage.

ISBN 1903506 09 3 pb 256pp + 8 pp plate section £12.99

Rats, Bat and Strange Toilets – Travel Tips for Unusual Countries

by David Freemantle

An entertaining travel book with serious undertones. It offers a range of useful and occasionally useless tips, insights and advice for travellers.

Featured on BBC Radio 4 Excess Baggage and in The Times Travel Supplement.

1903506 21 1 pb 240pp £7.99